Freedom Prayer
Training Manual

Mike Riches

Freedom Prayer Training
Second Edition, 2024
© 2024 by SycPub Global, LLC.

Published by SycPub Global. All rights reserved. No part of this publication may be reproduced, stored in a retrieval system, or transmitted in any form by any means, electronic, mechanical, photocopy, recording or otherwise, without the prior permission of the publisher, except as provided by USA copyright law.

You cannot make changes.
You cannot make copies without written permission from SycPub Global.
Additional books can be purchased from SycPub Global by contacting info@sycamorecommission.org.

Scriptures marked ESV are from The Holy Bible, English Standard Version® (ESV®) © 2001 by Crossway, a publishing ministry of Good News Publishers. All rights reserved.

Scriptures marked NASB are taken from the NEW AMERICAN STANDARD BIBLE®, © 1960, 1962, 1963, 1968, 1971, 1972, 1973, 1975, 1977, 1995 by The Lockman Foundation. Used by permission.

Scriptures marked NIV taken from the Holy Bible, NEW INTERNATIONAL VERSION®.
© 1973, 1978, 1984 Biblica. Used by permission of Zondervan. All rights reserved. The "NIV" and "New International Version" trademarks are registered in the United States Patent and Trademark Office by Biblica. Use of either trademark requires the permission of Biblica.

Scriptures marked NKJV are taken from the New King James Version®. © 1982 by Thomas Nelson, Inc. Used by permission. All rights reserved.

Scriptures marked NLT are taken from the Holy Bible, New Living Translation, copyright 1996, 2004. Used by permission of Tyndale House Publishers, Inc., Wheaton, Illinois 60189. All rights reserved.

ISBN 978-0-9828756-9-8

Editorial: Arlyn Lawrence, Hilary Murdoch, Aaron Atkission
Graphic Design and Layout: Brianna Showalter
Book Packaging: Scribe Book Company

Printed and bound in the U.S.A.

To Order:
www.sycamorecommission.org
info@sycamorecommission.org

Published by:

PO Box 158
Gig Harbor, WA 98335
USA

CONTENTS

PREFACE [5]
INTRODUCTION [7]

SESSION ONE
Foundations to Freedom Prayer Ministry [10]

SESSION TWO
Practicalities of Freedom Prayer Ministry [25]

SESSION THREE
Breaking into Freedom, Strongholds, and the "4Rs" [40]

SESSION FOUR
Receiving and Handling Revelation [57]

SESSION FIVE
Practicum [66]

SESSION SIX
Closing out a Ministry Session [73]

SESSION SEVEN
Roots and Fruits of Spiritual Strongholds [87]

SESSION EIGHT
Strongholds of Injustice and Love Deficit [95]

SESSION NINE
Understanding and Attacking Generational Attachments [110]

SESSION TEN
Soul Ties [125]

SESSION ELEVEN
Curses [134]

SESSION TWELVE
Summary and Commissioning [146]

APPENDIX [148]
Strongholds Listed and Described [151]
ENDNOTES [155]
ABOUT THE AUTHOR [156]

PREFACE

Like most everything in life, there is a story behind the journey you are about to begin with this material. "Freedom prayer ministry" initially emerged from a context of life and ministry in the community of a local church—a church of which I was pastor for just under 25 years. Freedom prayer was not birthed as a theory. It emerged from life experience that drove us to the Scriptures to find out why and how such dramatic life change was possible. Through this ministry, many people experienced distinct and undeniable healing from the depths of their inner person, as well as various physical healings.

This dramatic life change was not limited to our own church. As time went on, word spread. People from around the United States and many parts of the world, representing diverse cultures and spiritual heritages, sought help and healing from the Lord through our growing prayer ministry. God's healing work transcended all diversity because the spiritual and practical truths we were learning and applying are universal. That means that what we experienced in that particular setting can be experienced in other settings—in other churches, other ministries, and other communities and nations.

But make no mistake: freedom prayer ministry is not simply about people getting sorted and feeling better about themselves. It is about preparing all of us for something greater than our individual selves. It is for the end goal of making us "fit for purpose"—that purpose being the Kingdom Mission of the Church. Jesus made it very clear that He was leaving His people on earth for the very same purpose for which His Father had sent Him to earth. He came to proclaim and demonstrate God's kingdom values and culture of life in the midst of Satan's domain of destruction and death. To continue Jesus' ministry requires that God's power and love be released in a supernatural manner. Such a release is only possible through lives that are increasingly living in God's freedom.

The truths distilled from those original experience(s) and on which this training manual is based are summarized in SycPub Global's *Living Set Free Course Manual* as well as my book *Living Free: Recovering God's Design for Your Life*. Both of these resources are prerequisites to this course, as is my book *Hearing God's Voice for Yourself and Others*, co-authored with Tom Jonez (SycPub Global).

I'm so glad you picked up this manual and are embarking on this journey with us. *Freedom Prayer Training* presents the truths offered in our other courses and resources in a way that allows them to be exercised practically and effectively in ministry to yourself and others. I am excited for you. As you diligently apply yourself, no doubt this will become one of the more significant investments of your life. The fruit will speak for itself!

Mike Riches

INTRODUCTION

Welcome! By opening this manual and joining up with others who are also in training to become freedom prayer team ministers, you are embarking on an exciting and significant journey!

The objective of "Freedom Prayer Ministry" training is to gain practical understanding and life application to the truths you learned in *Living Set Free* and *Hearing God's Voice*. You will find that training and serving in freedom prayer ministry is a practical and powerful venue in which to apply these biblical truths not only in your own life, but also in serving others.

It's important to keep these truths real and dynamic. We don't ever want to reduce these powerful biblical principles to simply a "program." While freedom prayer training can provide a powerful *model* for ministry, we have designed this curriculum to help people increasingly appropriate these truths as a *lifestyle*.

It also is important that this training be conducted in the context of community, such as in a local church or ministry where there can be spiritual oversight, direction, and protection. The protection, direction, and provision of spiritual leadership are extremely important to safeguard and guide this ministry and the people investing themselves in it.

Prayer ministry is not an end in and of itself; its purpose must be rooted in the context of the Church's mission. The reason believers remain on earth in communities of the Church (i.e., in local churches and other ministries) is to fulfill the mission for which Jesus commissioned us. As God sent Jesus into the world, Jesus also commissions His disciples into the world, and for the same reason. The Church exists on earth to do the very works that Jesus demonstrated in the gospels.

John 17:18, 20 (NLT)
As you sent me into the world, I have sent them into the world...My prayer is not for them alone. I pray also for those who will believe in me through their message.

John 20:21 (NLT)
Again Jesus said, "Peace be with you! As the Father has sent me, I am sending you."

Jesus always ministered as He heard from the Father. Whether it was to teach, minister healing or deliverance, respond to the Pharisees, or choose His disciples, He listened to and obeyed the Father. In the same way, as believing followers of Jesus Christ, we are to be prepared, equipped, and fit to carry out the same ministry as Jesus.

The problem is that most people—if they were directed by God to pray healing for a person, minister deliverance, give a prophetic word, or share the Gospel—would be impeded from doing so by obstructions in their lives. Some of these issues might be things like fear, insignificance, unbelief, shame, rebellion, or pride. Freedom prayer ministry helps us identify and root out these spiritual strongholds so that followers of Jesus can be more and more freed up, fit, and equipped to move in the radical obedience and power necessary to accomplish Jesus' ministry in this world.

The following diagram illustrates how this process looks in real life. The first vertical bar on the left depicts Jesus living His life. He heard and obeyed the Father, doing the Father's works (Jn. 3:34, 6:38). As He did, He was destroying the works of Satan's kingdom (1 Jn. 3:8).

Jesus	Disciples	Disciples	Disciples
Jesus Ministry	**Freedom Prayer**	**Jesus' Image**	**Jesus Ministry**
Hearing & Obeying the Father; Destroying Satan's Works; Demonstrating God's Kingdom	Sin & Strongholds Obstruct Disciples from Hearing & Obeying Like Jesus	Increased Freedom, Christ-likeness, Obedience & Power	Doing Jesus' Works

The second vertical bar represents us, His disciples. We typically don't carry out the ministry of Jesus like He did, nor do we generally hear and obey like Jesus did. There are sins and strongholds that obstruct us. Appropriating the truths learned in *Living Set Free* helps set us free from those sins and strongholds. Exercising these truths through freedom prayer provides ministry to help God's people quickly and powerfully experience this freedom.

> Be mindful of your own ongoing need for restoration as you endeavor to minister restoration to others through freedom prayer ministry.

The third vertical bar depicts us, God's people, increasingly being set free from sin and strongholds as we appropriate biblical truths through freedom prayer. We begin to experience liberation from strongholds, as well as increased Christ-likeness, obedience, and power. This leads to the final vertical bar that shows us increasingly living out the life and ministry of Jesus.

As you embark on this course, we urge you to be mindful of your own ongoing need for restoration at the same time as you are endeavoring to minister to others through freedom prayer ministry. One of the biggest mistakes we've seen in this ministry is that of people too readily turning the focus to other people's restoration and, in the process, neglecting their own. The best posture to have is that of "restored restorer"—one who is continually and actively examining himself (or herself), and continuing in the freedom process in his (or her) own life.

This process never ends—at least, it won't until we see Jesus face to face and are perfectly conformed to His image (1 Jn. 3:2). But until then, we can rejoice that He has given us biblical tools and divinely powerful weapons, along with gifts of the Holy Spirit and His own authority, to help us be restored to our original design, continue the ministry He left for us to do, and advance His kingdom on earth.

Freedom prayer ministry is an important component of learning to appropriate and apply our God-given spiritual resources in our own lives and in the communities in which God has placed us. Your training can enable you to confidently and powerfully align yourself with Jesus' own mission statement, "to proclaim freedom for the prisoners and recovery of sight for the blind, to release the oppressed, to proclaim the year of the Lord's favor" (Lk. 4:18-19).

So, are you ready? Let's get started!

{ SESSION ONE }
FOUNDATIONS TO FREEDOM PRAYER MINISTRY

The Spirit of the Lord is upon me, for He has appointed me to preach Good News to the poor. He has sent me to proclaim that captives will be released, that the blind will see, that the downtrodden will be freed from their oppressors, and that the time of the Lord's favor has come.
Luke 4:18-19 NLT

Prayer is a multi-faceted component of the Christian life. For one, it is our communication vehicle with our Heavenly Father. It is a primary means by which we hear His voice, communicate our needs to Him, and minister His love and power to other people.

"Freedom prayer" is an applied spiritual and practical process by which we appropriate the particular biblical truths necessary to help people identify and root out spiritual strongholds from their lives. Freedom prayer, in summary, is:

- a practical expression of Jesus' mission statement: "to proclaim freedom for the prisoners and recovery of sight for the blind, to release the oppressed, to proclaim the year of the Lord's favor" (Lk. 4:18-19)

- a venue for receiving valuable revelation from the Holy Spirit yourself and through other believers, to help identify where Satan has established strongholds of rejection and wrong thinking (love and truth deficits, injustices, etc.)

- a process for helping people break free from spiritual bondages, curses, and generational strongholds that have kept them locked down and captive to sin

- a vehicle for exercising the authority we have in Christ over all the power of the enemy (Lk. 10:19)
- an opportunity for ministering in and imparting the power of the Holy Spirit to others in healing, prophetic ministry, and other spiritual gifts

The real goal of freedom prayer is "restoration"—being restored to God's original design for us. What the devil has tried to "steal, kill, and destroy" in our lives (Jn. 10:10), we can recover by the faith, authority, and power that come through Jesus. We can live in the joy and freedom of God's design as we become increasingly conformed to the image of Jesus Christ. Even more rewarding and exciting is to minister in this way to others through the gifts and power that are yours in Jesus Christ.

BRIEF OVERVIEW OF FREEDOM PRAYER

STEP ONE: ORIGINAL DESIGN

The ultimate goal of freedom prayer ministry is restoration to God's original design. Every person has an original design for his or her life, including purpose, attributes, and unique characteristics that make him or her both special and significant in God's plan and Kingdom.

It is powerful for a person to begin the restoration process by gaining a perspective of God's love, and an accurate view of how He regards him or her. In "original design" prayer, we ask the Holy Spirit to reveal to the prayer team specific aspects of how God created the person for whom we are praying (the "prayer candidate"). We would expect to hear character qualities, words of encouragement and hope, ways the person will contribute to God's Kingdom, and unique characteristics of his or her original design. We pray in this way with the conviction that God creates all people with design and purpose. Each and every person is significant.

STEP TWO: IDENTIFY STRONGHOLDS AND SIN'S TOPOS

After receiving a glimpse of God's "original design" for the prayer candidate, the second step in freedom prayer identifies intrusions of strongholds, sins, injustices, and other schemes of Satan's kingdom that prevent him or her from living in the fullness of life God designs for His people. These are identified through observation and prophetic ministry, with an emphasis placed on hearing God's voice in prayer.

4 Authority, Power, and Walking in Freedom
3 Repentance
2 Identify Strongholds and Sin's *Topos*
1 Original Design

> **FREEDOM PRAYER IS NOT ANOTHER COUNSELING MODEL.**

STEP THREE: REPENTANCE

After identifying these intrusions or "core strongholds," the prayer team leads the candidate through the process of repentance. Included in the candidate's repentance prayer is granting and receiving forgiveness as necessary, confessing recognized sin and related strongholds, vocally resisting and rebuking associated evil spirits, and verbal declarations replacing lies with truth. The prayer candidate actively receives God's forgiveness and resolutely determines to walk in the opposite spirit of attitude and action to the sin or stronghold addressed in the prayer time.

STEP FOUR: AUTHORITY, POWER, AND WALKING IN FREEDOM

A crucial component of this process is the prayer candidate taking responsibility for the sin strongholds in his or her life and exercising Christ's authority over them. He actively takes part in beginning to walk in personal freedom, sanctification, and God's power. This includes the infilling of God's Spirit and prayers of impartation by the prayer team, to enable and empower him or her to live life in God's love, strength, and truth.

RESTORATION THROUGH SPIRITUAL TRANSACTION

Freedom prayer ministry training is not intended to be another counseling model; rather, it is designed to help people identify and appropriate spiritual truths that result in spiritual transactions.

As you learned in the *Living Set Free* course, a "spiritual transaction" is in some ways similar to a business transaction. When two parties agree to transact an agreement, they align their agreement with appropriate laws. At that point a representative government official witnesses and authorizes the signatures, and confirms that an official transaction has taken place.

Freedom prayer IS NOT:

- merely talking about and analyzing a situation or "issue"
- behavior modification
- self-improvement

Freedom prayer IS:

- making real spiritual transactions that bring us into alignment with God's truth

Similarly, when a person receives Jesus Christ as his or her personal Lord and Savior, a spiritual transaction takes place. That person's life comes into alignment or agreement with God's truth. This includes the person recognizing his or her very real derelict condition before God due to sin, and understanding that salvation from sin can only be gained through faith in the life, death, and resurrection of Jesus Christ.

At this point, when a person's life is aligned with these truths in belief and conviction, and he declares through spoken words in prayer that he wants to receive the free gift of salvation from sin and become a child of God, the transaction is sealed by the power of God (Rom. 10:9). We see the effect of this transaction in the natural realm (2 Cor. 5:17). The person becomes fundamentally changed, a new creation. This is due to a spiritual transaction in the heavenlies which had a very real effect in the natural realm. This was a transaction of redemption!

The same thing happens in each one of our lives as we progress in exercising God's truth and power. When we pray prayers of repentance, declaration, spiritual authority, and faith, a real spiritual transaction takes place that will have natural realm effects.

Through training, you will become increasingly aware of the realities of the "heavenlies" (the spiritual realm). You will learn to recognize more and more distinctly how the heavenlies and natural realm interface in life. Merely talking about a situation does not bring a spiritual transaction and life change. What is required is:

- identifying biblical truth related to our life situation
- aligning ourselves with the truth in mind, will, emotions, words, and actions
- applying distinct spiritual principles of repentance
- granting and receiving forgiveness
- resisting and rebuking the minions of Satan's kingdom
- making declarations of obedience and applications of truth in our life
- praying to receive an infilling of God's Holy Spirit to live the God-empowered life

Freedom prayer is not about psychoanalysis, behavior modification, or spiritualized humanistic self-improvement. Nor is it intended to be a Christianized rendition of Freud, Jung, or Fromm. Freedom prayer is spiritual transaction through practical and powerful appropriation of God's truth. Jesus boldly stated that if we experientially understand, know, and live the truth, the truth will set us free!

God does what He has promised to do → SPIRITUAL TRANSACTION → **God's power released**

We do what we are responsible to do → SPIRITUAL TRANSACTION → **Natural realm effects observed**

John 8:31-32 (NLT)
Jesus said to the people who believed in him, "You are truly my disciples if you remain faithful to my teachings. And you will know the truth, and <u>the truth will set you free</u>" (emphasis added).

DEPENDENCE UPON GOD AND HIS POWER

God's authority and power are required to minister through freedom prayer. While we are responsible to exercise ourselves in God's gifts, grace, and truths, God's power is required to minister and bring true spiritual transaction. If God's power is not realized, the ministry time will be either boring or a mess. We need to engage a "human-divine cooperative."

The "human-divine cooperative" refers to people partnering with God by initiating what we can (and are responsible to) do, and then witnessing God doing what only He can do. Recall the story of Moses leading the Israelites across the Red Sea in Exodus 14.

Moses did not have the power in and of himself to part the Red Sea. Yet God would not part the sea until Moses initiated the faith to step out into what God had directed him to do. He had to raise his staff over the Red Sea before God would part it for the people to cross.

Freedom prayer will require many faith steps, both on your behalf and on the part of the people to whom you are ministering. This ministry is dependent on prophecy, discernment, wisdom, and other spiritual gifts being exercised by those on the prayer team. It requires God's Holy Spirit and power. It is an example of a human-divine cooperative in which the Holy Spirit in His power brings the revelation necessary for the recipient to receive healing, deliverance, and/or freedom.

> *If God's power is not realized, the ministry time will be either boring or a mess. We need to engage a "human-divine cooperative."*

1 Corinthians 4:19-20 (ESV)
But I will come to you soon, if the Lord wills, and I will find out not the talk of these arrogant people but their power. For the kingdom of God does not consist in talk but in power.

OUR POSTURE IN FREEDOM PRAYER

THE PRAYER MINISTRY TEAM'S RESPONSIBILITY

It is important to keep in mind that the opportunity to minister in (and receive) freedom prayer is a privilege, not an entitlement. Though we have the assurance that we can come "boldly" and "confidently" before the throne of grace (Heb. 4:16), we never want to do so presumptuously. The more we can be in alignment with God's truths and heart, the greater He is able to move in and through us. With this in mind, we want to make sure we live prepared for ministry. This should include the following considerations:

HUMILITY

Whether on the giving or receiving end of freedom prayer ministry, our foundational posture must be true humility. The Scriptures make it clear that God does not move freely in the context of pride. God opposes the proud but gives His grace to the humble. Humility is seeing yourself as God does—in all of your significance and worth—yet conducting yourself as a servant, not lifting or appraising yourself above others. This was Jesus' attitude (Phil. 2:5-10).

Humility is a heart attitude that is demonstrated in practical ways, including:

- walking in forgiveness as a lifestyle
- being totally committed to God and advancing His Kingdom in heart and attitude
- being available for anything; being flexible
- being willing to serve versus being served
- surrendering entitlements, ambition, and desire for recognition
- submitting to the manner of prayer ministry established and desired by your church leadership
- working in mutual submission which allows the prayer team to minister in Spirit-led coordination
- directing attention to Jesus, not yourself
- being one who will not exhort someone to do what you yourself are not willing to do

Humility is a critical component of sharing revelation we have received with those to whom we are ministering. It is always important to offer the revelation humbly and ask if it resonates with them or if they recognize it in their lives. We must never force revelation or give people the impression that they do not have the option to question it or disagree.

James 4:6 (NIV)
But he gives us more grace. That is why Scripture says: "God opposes the proud but gives grace to the humble."

Philippians 2:3-4 (NIV)
Do nothing out of selfish ambition or vain conceit, but in humility consider others better than yourselves. Each of you should look not only to your own interests, but also to the interests of others.

> When we pray prayers of repentance, declaration, spiritual authority, and faith, spiritual transactions take place that will have natural realm effects.

LOVE

As with any other aspect of Jesus' ministry and Kingdom living, in freedom prayer ministry we must truly love others as God loves. We must see others with God's compassion—as Jesus sees them—and relate to them accordingly. We must see them not as they are, but as what they will become as they are transformed.

We represent God when we are ministering in His name, which means we also have to accurately represent His heart of love. Those who live and minister out of God's love will see themselves as servants of others. They will view themselves as vessels of His mercy, not His judgment.

It is important that people leave their prayer times feeling loved, not condemned. They need to experience the grace and love of God through us. We can ensure this happens by the way we direct the prayer times, share revelation, and react to what they share with us, as well as by prioritizing time for blessing and impartation at the end.

1 John 3:16, 18 (NLT)
We know what real love is because Jesus gave up his life for us. So we also ought to give up our lives for our brothers and sisters. Dear children, let's not merely say that we love each other; let us show the truth by our actions.

HOLINESS

By "holiness" we do not mean legislated righteousness or legalism. True holiness that is of God is liberating, filled with vibrant life and freedom. It means increasingly aligning our mindset, words, and actions with God's truths and heart. Primarily this entails making sure we are addressing known and volitional sin.

We cannot take lightly the need for those engaged in freedom prayer ministry to be continuously and actively engaged in their own restoration/sanctification process. True authenticity and anointing is dependent on it. We are never "finished," at least, not until we see Jesus face to face!

Out of your own freedom process, you will be able to relate to those who come to you for prayer. Your story or testimony of restoration, when strategically and concisely shared, can be used greatly by God for those to whom you will be ministering. Always remember: You cannot impart to others what you are not allowing God to do in you.

Psalm 66:18 (ESV)
If I had cherished iniquity in my heart, the Lord would not have listened.

1 Peter 1:15-16 (ESV)
But as he who called you is holy, you also be holy in all your conduct, since it is written, "You shall be holy, for I am holy."

FAITH

The Scriptures clearly state that faith is critical in God's power being released. Conversely, unbelief will inhibit God's power being released. Faith, simply stated, is stepping out in obedience to God with a confidence that God will be faithful to His word, truth, and character. In His faithfulness to Himself, He will be faithful to you as you step out in faithful obedience.

Always remember: You cannot impart to others what you are not allowing God to do in you.

Hebrews 11:1, 6 (ESV)
Now faith is the assurance of things hoped for, the conviction of things not seen. And without faith it is impossible to please him, for whoever would draw near to God must believe that he exists and that he rewards those who seek him.

Mark 6:5-6 (NLT)
And because of their unbelief, he couldn't do any miracles among them except to place his hands on a few sick people and heal them. And he was amazed at their unbelief. Then Jesus went from village to village, teaching the people.

HOLY SPIRIT FILLING

Holy Spirit filling is necessary for us to move and minister in God's power. Jesus did His mighty works being filled with the Holy Spirit. He instructed and modeled this truth for His disciples so they would carry out His kingdom work in God's power. (For more teaching on the in-filling of the Holy Spirit, review Section Two in the *Living Set Free Course Manual*, or Chapter 7 in *Living Free: Recovering God's Design for Your Life*).

Acts 10:38 (NLT)
And you know that God anointed Jesus of Nazareth with the Holy Spirit and with power. Then Jesus went around doing good and healing all who were oppressed by the devil, for God was with him.

Acts 4:30-31 (NLT)
Stretch out your hand with healing power; may miraculous signs and wonders be done through the name of your holy servant Jesus." After this prayer, the meeting place shook, and they were all filled with the Holy Spirit. Then they preached the word of God with boldness.

PROPERLY ALIGNED IN GOD'S GOVERNMENT

God's government is very important to God and should therefore be important to us. God is the ultimate Authority and has extended His authority on earth through offices of governing responsibility in people, such as civil and governmental leaders, parents, husbands, church leaders, employers/supervisors, etc. To not be in an attitude of proper alignment with authority could put us in a posture of insubordination or independence. At the very least, rebellion of heart puts us in a strained relationship with God.

Alignment with God's government includes submissive attitudes and actions in relationship to all those in authority to you, especially as you function in prayer ministry as an extension and under the authority of the pastors, elders, or leadership team in your church. The realm of the heavenlies knows, understands, and operates according to spiritual authority. If you are out of proper alignment, you are at great risk of compromising God's power in your life to carry out the necessary ministry. You need to be accountable to pastoral leadership, and to the leadership of the ministry in which you are operating.

More specifically, as it relates to freedom prayer ministry, the prayer team needs to submit to the authority of the person leading the prayer time. This is explained further in a later session.

1 Peter 2:13-17 (NIV)
Submit yourselves for the Lord's sake to every authority instituted among men: whether to the king, as the supreme authority, or to governors, who are sent by him to punish those who do wrong and to commend those who do right. For it is God's will that by doing good you should silence the ignorant talk of foolish men. Live as free men, but do not use your freedom as a cover-up for evil; live as servants of God. Show proper respect to everyone; Love the brotherhood of believers, fear God, honor the king.

> Alignment with God's government includes submissive attitudes and actions in relationship to all those in authority to you.

Hebrews 13:17 (NLT)
Obey your spiritual leaders and do what they say. Their work is to watch over your souls, and they know they are accountable to God. Give them reason to do this joyfully and not with sorrow. That would certainly not be for your benefit.

Independence/Rebellion
- not in alignment with authority
- not under Godly covering
- unprotected and vulnerable
- God's power is hindered

In submission to leadership
- in alignment
- under cover
- protected
- God's power can be released

THE RECIPIENT'S POSTURE

SALVATION

First, the person receiving prayer must be a believing follower of Jesus Christ, having received salvation. This is not to say we don't ever pray for those who don't yet know Christ as their Savior. However, freedom prayer by its nature is a ministry that can only be appropriated by those who have already become children of God through faith in Christ. (We will specifically address this issue later in the course, along with how to minister in a prayer session if the candidate is not a believer in Jesus and does not wish to become one.)

HUNGER

Secondly, a person receiving ministry must genuinely desire to receive prayer and have asked for it. If the person is not desirous, hungry, and desperate for the ministry time, significant spiritual transaction won't happen. While the person might be somewhat unsettled or nervous if he or she has not received ministry in this way before, there should still be a recognized measure of humility and hunger in desiring ministry.

RESPONSIBILITY

The person also must be willing to take responsibility for his or her own freedom and restoration. If at any time in the process the candidate resists or refuses to respond to truth that has been presented in love, you cannot go further in the prayer session. This can often be evidenced in areas where forgiveness needs to be granted and/or received, or where true repentance is necessary but to which the person will not submit.

If it comes to a point where you feel you cannot go further in a prayer session due to this, you may wish to listen to the Holy Spirit for words of comfort, strength, and encouragement, which is a goal of prophetic ministry (1 Cor. 14:30). You may choose to pray for words of blessing, or for the candidate's original design. We want every person receiving prayer to leave feeling loved, encouraged, and positive towards the session so they are inclined to come back for further prayer in the future.

THE EXERCISE: Praying for "Original Design"

CONDUCTING A FREEDOM PRAYER SESSION – PRAYING FOR GOD'S ORIGINAL DESIGN

When we pray for a person's original design, we ask the Holy Spirit to reveal aspects of how God has created him or her. For example, we might receive that a young man has a heart of compassion, is a courageous leader, loves to worship, has a father's heart, and loves to see God in nature. We might receive that a woman was created with a unique capacity for laughter and joy, is creative and musical, has a heart for the poor, and is spiritually gifted with wisdom and healing. (NOTE: A description of John the Baptist's "original design" is in Luke 1:13-17 as a model.) We are NOT giving the person direction for life or telling him or her what to do (e.g., "You should be doing the children's ministry at church," or "You should go to Africa to be a missionary.") The revelation should be quite general and always encouraging, to build the person up.

In your first prayer team training session, you will work with an experienced prayer team minister(s). There will be at least one (maybe two) experienced prayer team member(s) in your group of four. One of the experienced members will lead or "captain" the time. The others submit to the captain's direction and act as "listeners." Two people in the group will receive prayer concerning God's original design for them. When you are not receiving prayer, you will join in on the prayer time with the experienced prayer ministers to pray for another trainee. The prayer time should proceed as follows:

STEP ONE: THE TEAM ENSURES IT IS READY TO PRAY

(Note: This step should be done discreetly prior to the prayer time, in such a way that the person receiving prayer does feel not awkward.)

The captain should inquire, *"Lord, are there any issues with us as individuals, or as a team, which need to be addressed and cleared up so we are free to hear Your voice and minister?"*

The captain will discern if the team should deal with any issues revealed quietly in their hearts, if he or she should pray aloud on behalf of everyone, or if each person should pray very briefly out loud.

A sample response might be, if the team were to receive that "fear" was an issue: *"Lord, I/we repent of any fear of not hearing Your voice. I/we receive Your forgiveness. In Jesus' name I/we rebuke any spirit of fear from this prayer time. I/we replace fear with total trust in God, and confidence that He will speak to me/us for His glory today."*

STEP TWO: THE CAPTAIN EXERCISES AUTHORITY OVER THE PRAYER TIME

- Ask God to seal off the environment and the prayer time with His presence so that His work is done without being compromised by the enemy.
- Thank the Lord for the prayer candidate by name.
- Affirm in faith that God's work will be done and that you are coming into this time on the basis of God's love and authority.
- Take authority, in Jesus' name, over any influence of the enemy that would compromise the prayer session in any specific or general ways.
- Take authority over any human imagination, emotions, logic, and fleshly ideas not generated by God, forbidding them from coming into the time. (Note that we do not want to completely bind our imaginations and emotions, as the Holy Spirit often uses them to speak to us. However, we DO want to bind the enemy from using them against us or energizing them in any way.)

For example: *"In Jesus Christ's name, I bind any influence of the enemy that might seek to disrupt this prayer time. I specifically bind any spirit of confusion and fear, and command it to leave this place right now. I bind any demonic spirit from influencing our imaginations and emotions in any way, and submit them, Holy Spirit, to Your use and Your use alone."*

STEP THREE: THE TEAM INQUIRES OF THE LORD FOR ORIGINAL DESIGN

The captain will ask the following questions of the Lord in prayer (simultaneously):

"Lord, what characteristics or components did You create as a part of _____'s life? Generally speaking, how have You created _____ to contribute to this world and/or Your kingdom?"

If time allows, the captain can ask a third question, *"Father, how do You see this person at this time?"*

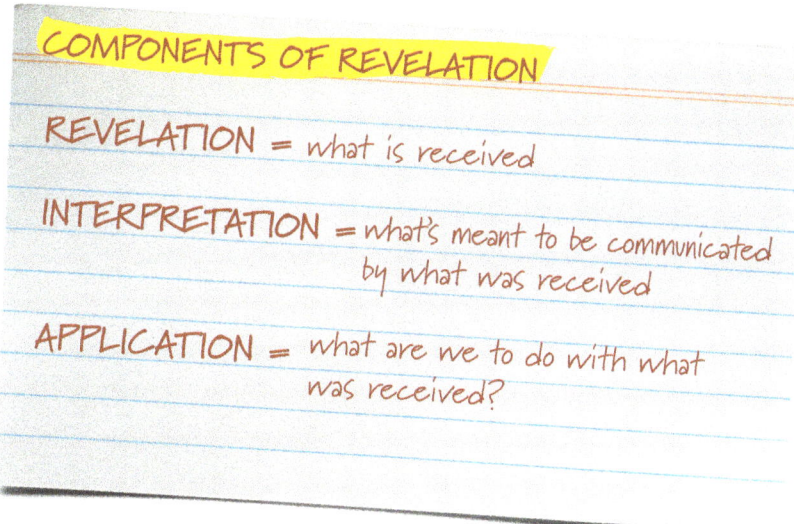

Each person on the prayer team should listen quietly for the Holy Spirit's response and write down on a pad of paper what he/she receives. These may be words, mental pictures, impressions, and/or Scriptures. Pass these to the captain for him/her to discern what should (or should not) be shared at this time, and how it should be shared with the candidate. (The captain may have each person on the team share individually with the candidate, or he/she may decide to present it all at once himself/herself.)

STEP FOUR: CLOSE IN PRAYER

Encourage the prayer candidate to claim the truths for himself or herself (e.g. *"Thank you, Lord, that You have made me a woman of compassion and courage…"*). Then pray a prayer of blessing over him or her. Include specific original design truths received, thanking God for how He has made the candidate. Ask for the Holy Spirit to empower him or her to grow in those things.

NOTE:

Two people in each group should receive prayer for his or her "original design" in this first session. The total time of this exercise for each person should not take more than 25 to 30 minutes so that two persons can receive prayer in this exercise hour.

AT-HOME ASSIGNMENT

1. Thoroughly re-read this session after having prayed with your team and a prayer candidate for the candidate's original design. Make notes in the margins on points you want to review or emphasize for next time, or about questions you'd like to ask.

2. Read the next session (Session Two: Practicalities of Freedom Prayer Ministry) before the next class.

3. Personally work through the strongholds assigned by your instructor in SycPub Global's *Walking in Freedom* manual or in the *Living Set Free Course Manual*. Begin to familiarize yourself with the concepts and vocabulary related to the various stronghold issues listed in the manual and which are commonly encountered in freedom prayer ministry.

4. Be mindful of your own ongoing need for restoration as you study and meditate on these truths. We always want to operate from a platform of humility and a posture of "me, too" as we minister to one another.

{ SESSION TWO }
PRACTICALITIES OF FREEDOM PRAYER MINISTRY

Do nothing out of selfish ambition or vain conceit, but in humility consider others better than yourselves. Each of you should look not only to your own interests, but also to the interests of others. Your attitude should be the same as that of Christ Jesus.
Philippians 2:3-5 NIV

When ministering to people in freedom prayer, it is important to interact with them in an understanding way. Keep in mind that they are probably feeling somewhat on edge and nervous. We want to assure them from the outset that, in this prayer session, they will experience:

- people who love Jesus
- people who love them
- an outpouring of God's love that will flow through the prayer team to them

We have all experienced being in a new or unfamiliar environment at one time or another. Most of us feel a bit awkward and uncomfortable in such circumstances. That's why a very important aspect of this ministry is your reassurance to the people receiving prayer, helping them feel comfortable and relaxed.

Ultimately, we want a prayer candidate to finish the ministry time feeling loved with Jesus' love, and experiencing spiritual transaction that changes his or her life. With that objective in mind, in this session we will cover:

- some basic, "common sense" suggestions for putting people at ease, minimizing distractions, and creating a warm, loving, and effective atmosphere for a freedom prayer session

- the composition of the ministry team along with the positions and roles of the members on a team
- practicalities of how to relate sensitively, safely, and in an orderly manner

THE MINISTRY TEAM – POSITIONS, ROLES, AND GIFTS

For the ministry prayer time to be as effective as possible (i.e., real spiritual transactions are realized and the person receives a transformational experience of God's truth and love), a "team" functioning in a Holy Spirit-filled manner is crucial. The team needs to be operating according to both particular roles and spiritual gifting.

TEAM POSITIONS

A prayer team is usually made up of three people (a "captain" and two "listeners"). Sometimes, however, a team may just be two people (captain and listener). One advantage of utilizing three people is the opportunity for a less experienced listener to join an experienced team for training purposes.

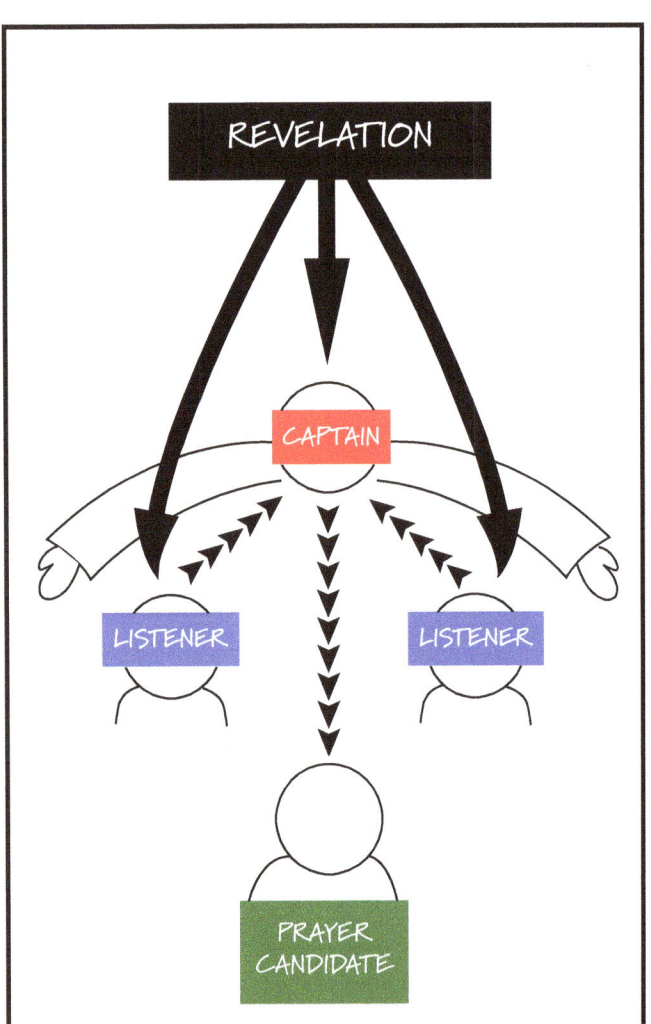

THE CAPTAIN

The "captain" is the leader of the team and should be gifted with a measure of leadership, wisdom, and discernment.

Captains are responsible for keeping the session in order, seeing the "big picture," recognizing the spiritual principles operating, and for directing and stewarding the revelation received in the prayer time. They will have had some experience of ministering in freedom prayer, having served as a listener before participating as a captain. Captains should also have a growing grasp of the Scriptures and biblical truth. Scriptural truth and its biblical principles connected with relevant application are critical in order for spiritual transactions to take place. It is the experiential knowledge of truth that sets people free (Jn. 8:31-32).

LISTENER(S)

This person is responsible for listening for and hearing from the Lord in prayer, and sharing with the captain what he/she receives. Listeners are generally those who have a measure of prophetic gifting. However, knowing that all children of God hear from Him, even if you do not feel you have a particular gifting in the prophetic, remember that we all have the grace of hearing God's voice. We can all learn to be "listeners." Additionally, spiritual gifts of discernment, wisdom, helps, knowledge, and mercy are beneficial gifts for this position and role on the team.

COACH/OVERSEER

In a training session or large group of many teams ministering, this person is available to prayer teams on-site as needed for wisdom, revelation, discernment, and practical support. A coach typically will be very experienced in freedom prayer ministry and able to troubleshoot and train others in a ministry setting.

ROLES

NOTE: It is important for prayer ministry teams to function under the spiritual authority of the leadership of their church or the ministry of which they are a part. They are an extension of such leadership and represent them as they represent the Lord.

The Captain's Role

The ministry begins with and is facilitated by the "captain," for the sake of order and to minimize confusion. The following are some of the characteristics of the captain's role:

DIRECTS THE TIME

- **prepares the team, sets the spiritual tone of the session, and directs the prayer time** from start to finish, making sure all components are thoroughly covered
- **responsible for ensuring the prayer candidate is cared for and ministered to.** He or she is the primary communicator with the candidate on behalf of the team.
- **manages the time and pace of the session,** making sure it does not get bogged down and that everything is handled thoroughly. If the session gets off track or the prayer candidate wants to dominate the direction of the prayer time, the captain is responsible for getting things back on track.
- **asks the questions in prayer** when seeking prophetic revelation from the Lord
- seeks the wisdom and insight of the other team members, but **is ultimately responsible to make all necessary decisions as to how best to proceed**
- **hears from the Lord along with the rest of the team.** This is partly how he or she will know how to proceed, what questions to ask, and which revelation should be shared (or not). However, the captain's *primary* role is directing the action.

Time is crucial and spiritual transaction in prayer must take precedence over conversation.

ENSURES THERE IS CLARITY AND ORDER

- **makes sure the prayer candidate understands** what is happening and what to expect
- **organizes and strategically shares the revelation, discernment, and wisdom of the team** with the person receiving ministry
- **ensures the rest of the prayer team has clarity about what is expected of them**—for example, giving direction about whether revelation should be written down and passed to the captain, or shared directly with the candidate
- **keeps clear, legible, summarized notes of the revelation** as shared by the prayer team and then confirmed or expanded upon by the prayer candidate during the course of the prayer time. These notes can be given to the person after the session.

MOVES THE PRAYER CANDIDATE TOWARD SPIRITUAL TRANSACTION

- **shares with the prayer candidate what has been received by the team.** This is to be done with love and explanation as necessary.
- **ensures the prayer time stays in the realm of prayer** and spiritual transaction, and is not reduced to a counseling session or a discussion of personal experience and wisdom
- **assists in leading the prayer candidate through the personal revelation** (primarily through questions). People who are operating out of strongholds are often unaware of their bondage. It is their worldview and/or only experience of life—it is their "normal!" Asking questions is one way to stimulate possible understanding or revelation as to what was received by the prayer team.
- **leads the prayer candidate in spiritual transaction.** The captain may offer to lead the person in prayer, line by line. Or, if the person understands the principles and has had some freedom prayer before, the captain may simply need to prompt him or her with a summary of what to cover at each stage, prompting gently if something is left out.

The Listener's Role

The listener's primary role is to listen to the Lord on behalf of the prayer candidate and to intercede throughout the prayer time. The following are some aspects of the "listener's" role:

- **submits to and follows the leadership of the captain.** (This is essential for a smooth running prayer session and has a very real spiritual impact on the session. Even if the listener disagrees with how the captain is leading the session, he/she needs to submit to the captain's delegated authority in this setting. If necessary, a discussion can be had afterwards for mutual benefit and learning.)
- **receives prophetic disclosure or revelation from the Lord on behalf of the prayer candidate**

- **relays revelation, discernment, discernment of spirits, impressions, wisdom,** etc. to the captain, in the format the captain has requested. (If the listener receives additional revelation while the captain is leading prayer, the listener should not interrupt but discreetly write on a piece of paper and offer it to the captain.)

- **offers revelation to the captain humbly and with an "open-handed" attitude,** not taking offense if the captain discerns not to share it. (A listener should not be disappointed if the person receiving prayer does not recognize or accept the revelation. The responsibility is completed once he or she has heard from the Lord and shared it with the captain.)

- **keeps clear, legible notes of the revelation received,** as directed by the captain. (It can be helpful to write original design/blessings on a separate sheet from strongholds/roots, in case the captain decides only to give certain elements of the revelation to the prayer candidate.)

- **communicates to the person receiving ministry** under the coordination of the captain

- **silently intercedes for the person receiving prayer** as the captain leads him or her in prayer

- **seeks to be sensitive to the spiritual atmosphere in the prayer time** and silently takes authority over any scheme of the enemy where necessary—for example, binding a spirit of confusion or fear, or interceding for wisdom and discernment for the captain

- **prays prayers of impartation and blessing over the candidate** at the end of the session. (The listener may receive specific words, pictures, or Scriptures during the prayer time, which can be noted and then shared/prayed at the end.)

> The listener's primary role is to listen to the Lord on behalf of the prayer candidate and to intercede throughout the prayer time.

When we pray with and are mutually submitted to other believers, we can benefit from some of the spiritual gifts that operate in the Church.

SPIRITUAL GIFTS

Spiritual gifts are supernatural capacities for ministry that every follower of Jesus Christ has. Each believer receives spiritual gifts from the Holy Spirit when he or she becomes a part of the family of God, the Body of Christ (1 Cor. 12:7). These gifts are for the purpose of strengthening the Body, giving power for doing Jesus' ministry, and advancing the Kingdom of God on earth. Not all of the gifts are specifically related to prayer, prophecy, and/or hearing God's voice. However, they do play an integral role in operating in this capacity.

When we pray with and are mutually submitted to other believers, here's how we can benefit from some of the spiritual gifts that operate in the Church:

Prophecy – someone receives specific and timely communication from the Lord, primarily an immediate, spontaneous message or revelation

Knowledge – someone has a supernaturally high degree of understanding of the Scriptures and their particular relevance to people and situations. (Sometimes this gift is ascribed to the ability to receive spontaneous revelation about people and/or situations, but we would more readily describe such a gift in the realm of *prophecy*.)

Wisdom – someone has the supernatural ability to bring needed insight and/or practical application to a person or situation

Discernment – someone has a supernatural sensitivity to whether a person, message, or situation is being influenced by the Holy Spirit or by a demonic spirit, whether something is of the Lord—or not

Faith – someone can believe God's Word, character, and promises to a degree that surpasses "normal" human expectation and opens the door for God's power to flow in miraculous ways

Mercy – someone is able to supernaturally feel and extend the love and compassion of Christ to people who are in need of His touch on their lives and/or situations

Exhortation – someone is able to strongly encourage and motivate other people in applying spiritual truths and living in truth and righteousness

Healing – someone has an above-normal track record for praying for physical healing in others and seeing miraculous results

This is not an exhaustive list of possible spiritual gifts. It is rather just a sampling to give us a glimpse of the exponential benefits that come when we minister in community with other believers who are exercising a plurality of spiritual gifts.[1] The spiritual power of a team is maximized when the members of the team are operating under the control of the Holy Spirit, according to their spiritual gifting.

FREEDOM MINISTRY ETIQUETTE

BREAKING THE ICE

SMILE! Communicate warmly with your eyes.

Never underestimate the capacity and power of a natural and authentic smile; it communicates more than words. Make natural eye contact with the person to whom you are ministering, as much is communicated through your eyes. Also, as you make eye contact, note with discernment what you see in your prayer candidate's eyes; the Lord may speak to you through such observations.

Connect relationally with the person receiving prayer.

Typically time is at a premium in a freedom prayer session. You cannot afford to spend excessive time in conversation at this point, at the expense of the spiritual transaction of prayer. It is important, though, that to some degree you connect with the person at a relational level. This will pay dividends in the person feeling at ease and helping him or her be able to trust you and the process. This can be accomplished by finding some non-threatening common ground on which to get acquainted.

It is also helpful for the captain to ask what previous experience the person has had with Jesus-ministry truths, *Living Set Free* training, and/or freedom prayer. This will help you discern what can be covered in the prayer time, and what level of explanation may be needed.

Be natural and authentic. Don't over-spiritualize.

Helping restore God's people to His original design for them is NORMAL. It is very important that in every aspect of the ministry experience, your prayer candidate sees that relating to God, hearing His voice, and receiving His work in their lives are done in a very natural manner.

Communicate in such a way that you convey God's care and regard for the candidate.

God often uses people to communicate His love to His children (1 Jn. 4:12). As a representative of their Heavenly Father, be sensitive to any nervousness, discomfort, or awkwardness people might be feeling.

Determine to lavish God's love on your prayer candidate. Convey God's love and truth through your words, countenance, and actions. Try to communicate acceptance, compassion, and interest. Body posture should be casual, not too intense, and not overly "poker-faced." Validate the person by your body posture when the prayer candidate is praying or speaking, assuring him or her that you are listening (especially the "captain").

Make sure you have the person's name correct!

Using the person's name is crucial. Even more important is not getting the person's name *wrong*. It helps to say the name right away to impress it on your own mind. It is also helpful to write it across the top of your notepad.

Be able and prepared to share a brief testimony.

Share aspects of your own testimony of freedom and restoration. When you identify with a person in this way, it helps him recognize he is on common ground with you. This can help the prayer candidate realize he is on a journey like others—he is not unique in his ministry experience. However, since time is crucial and spiritual transaction in prayer must take precedence over conversation, keep any testimony extremely brief.

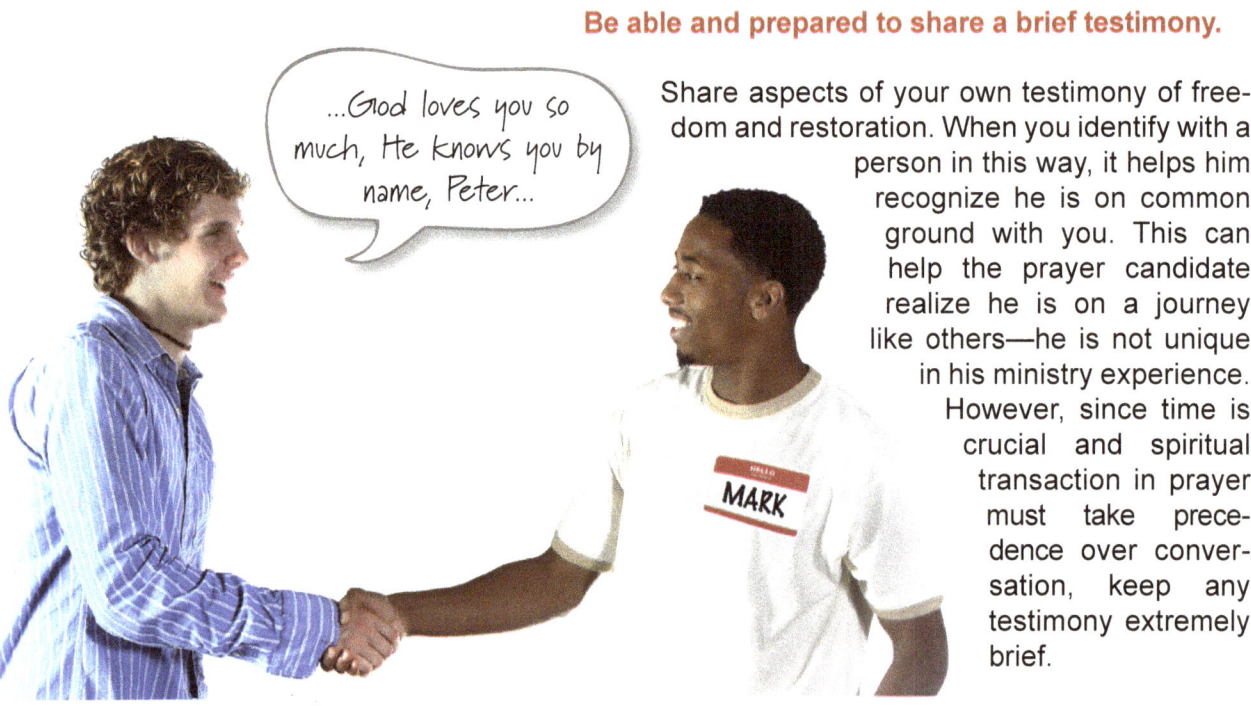

Discreetly bind any activity of the enemy immediately.

Binding demonic influence should always be part of your preparation for the ministry time. However, during the prayer time you may need to repeat it or more specifically exercise your authority, especially necessary if you identify a tangible spiritual influence trying to compromise the ministry time. This can be evidenced by the person seeming unduly agitated or being overly affected by fear, or if there is a high level of distraction.

Verbally summarize the process of the prayer time.

Part of helping the prayer candidate relax and gain the most benefit is informing him or her about what will comprise the prayer time. Clearly and concisely, the captain should explain what the prayer time will look like. As you explain each stage, make sure there is clarity at each point. If you believe further explanation is needed, take a brief moment to share a bit more detail. The more the candidate is aware of what is about to happen, the more relaxed he or she can be in the process. Use clear, plain language people can easily understand, even if they have not had previous experience with freedom prayer. Avoid religious terminology, jargon, or vocabulary that cannot be easily understood without explanation.

PRAYER TEAM ETIQUETTE

Present a neat and respectful appearance.

It is important to avoid sloppiness or overly casual attire (sweat pants, athletic shorts, etc.). These can be a distraction by conveying a lack of care. Likewise, it is important to dress modestly. Clothing should be comfortable and conservative. Women's clothes should fit fairly loosely and provide adequate coverage. Different people have different distraction levels, so gravitate to the conservative side of the spectrum.

Be conscious of personal hygiene.

Personal hygiene can be another significant distraction factor. While it may seem like common sense, it is not something we can take for granted. Be aware of breath (use breath mints or fresh gum if necessary), body odor, and the condition of your clothing and shoes.

Be aware of the atmosphere in the room, physically and spiritually.

Be alert to physical comfort levels of the area in which you are meeting. Is the air too warm, too cold, too stuffy, or too breezy? Is the seating and seating arrangement comfortable? Is water available for both the person receiving prayer and the prayer team? Are there tissues available?

Stay alert in your spirit to the spiritual environment as well. Are there confusion, jumbled thoughts, an air of antagonism, passivity, etc.? Such an environment is not of the Lord.

> Remember the importance of being pastoral, when needed, in your interaction with your prayer candidate.

James 3:17 (NLT)
But the wisdom that comes from heaven is first of all pure; then peace-loving, considerate, submissive, full of mercy and good fruit, impartial and sincere.

1 Corinthians 14:33 (NLT)
God is not a God of disorder but of peace.

Be alert to the state of the person to whom you are ministering. If he or she becomes agitated, overly emotional, hostile, or is excessively dwelling on sorrowful or angry thoughts, you are very possibly encountering the manifestation of a demonic spirit energizing him or her. Stop what you are doing and bind the enemy's activity that is compromising the prayer time. When it is necessary to exercise your spiritual authority, do it in a calm and assuring manner.

Use appropriate physical touch.

There are times when a touch is not only appropriate but necessary. It can be when a person is moved emotionally during the prayer time and needs comfort, or when the person simply needs to be strengthened with reassurance. Remember the importance of being pastoral in your interaction with your prayer candidate when needed, particularly the captain.

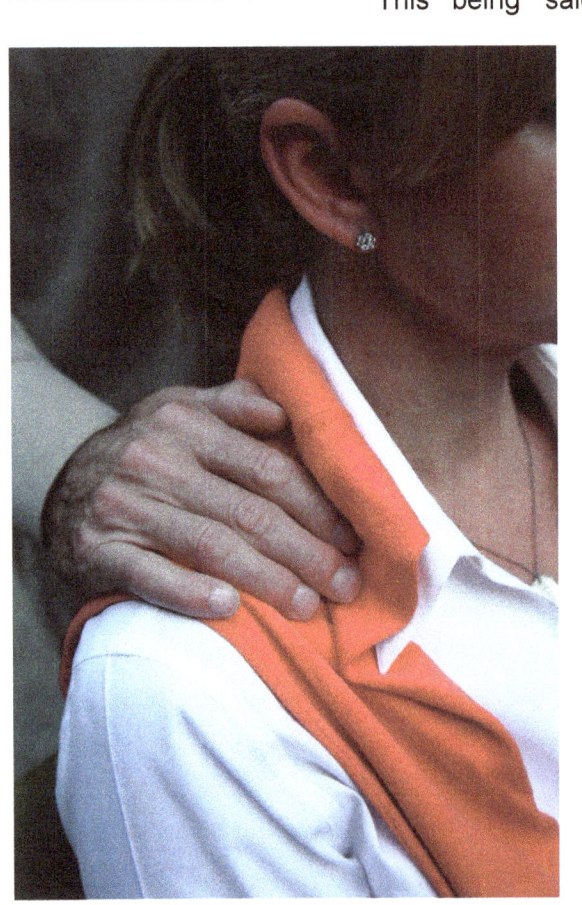

This being said, we need to make mention of some practical precautions. Be particularly cautious when ministering with the opposite gender. It is not that there can never be an appropriate touch between men and women in this setting, but always be mindful of the potential problems. Also, the person receiving ministry could feel uncomfortable with physical touch, especially if there have been abuse issues in his or her past.

When it is appropriate to provide a touch, be warm and genuine while avoiding anything that could possibly be misinterpreted. Simply placing a hand on the person's shoulder or arm can give significant comfort and can contribute toward significant spiritual transactions in the life of the person to whom you are ministering.

Additionally, during the impartation part of a prayer time, the "laying-on of hands" is an important part of releasing God's power and blessing to the person. During this part of the session, the captain should always ask the candidate whether he or she is comfortable with the prayer team placing a hand on his or her shoulder to pray.

Be sensitive to gender-specific issues.

It is best for spouses to minister together whenever possible. Understanding that this is not always possible, it is nonetheless important that the ministry team always include at least one person of the same gender as the person receiving prayer.

At times, certain gender-sensitive issues may surface during the ministry prayer time that might raise a certain level of discomfort for the person receiving ministry. While not always necessary, sometimes it is best for those on the team of the opposite gender to be dismissed for a period of time while the sensitive issue is addressed.

Let the Holy Spirit direct the prayer session.

Don't discount the prepared list of issues a person may bring, but neither allow it to direct the prayer time. The enemy generally hides under a smoke screen, and the person's perception of his or her issue(s) can be such a smoke screen. After all, the Scriptures warn us, "*The heart is deceitful above all things*" (Jer. 17:9).

Be mindful that often what gains the person's attention is symptomatic. What God really wants to address is the root of the issue(s). Look for ways to include the person's concerns as you address the issues the Lord reveals, but don't allow them to control the session.

OTHER PRACTICALITIES

Set-up

At each group of chairs for a prayer session, there should be the following:

- A pad of paper and pen for the captain and each listener, plus a spare pen
- Breath freshener, mints/gum
- Tissues
- Bibles
- Water—available for the prayer team and those receiving prayer

Putting Together Prayer Teams

The leaders of the church prayer ministry will need to prayerfully discern the make-up of the teams, including who should pray together, and who should captain and who should listen. This should be done with an awareness of individuals' strengths, weaknesses, and experience, but also by asking God for revelation. It is generally appropriate for people to receive additional training instruction before serving as captains.

> Guard against the temptation to tell others "testimonies" about what happened in prayer times.

Confidentiality—a Key Principle

The prayer team must be committed to the confidentiality of anything shared in the prayer time. The captain may wish to assure the candidate at the start of the time that this is the case. The team may even want to pray for "godly forgetfulness" at the end of the prayer time, praying that their minds do not hold onto the details of the prayer time. It is essential that we treat the person we prayed for with respect, grace, and ease when we next see them.

Guard especially against the temptation to relate "testimonies" about what happened in prayer times. If you feel that a particular testimony would be an encouragement to the church, ask the person who received prayer if he or she would be willing to give the testimony personally. If you want to share a testimony in a service or training session, even if it is shared anonymously, you should ask the permission of the person concerned.

If something is revealed by the prayer candidate within a prayer time that the captain feels must be shared with the leadership, he or she should inform the prayer candidate immediately, and give him or her the option of whether to continue sharing about the issue. This is obviously the case where a criminal situation is concerned, but also for situations concerning the safety of that person or others. The leadership of your church/prayer ministry should establish its own parameters for what those situations might be.

As you did last week, you will now work with an experienced prayer team minister(s). There will be at least one (maybe two) experienced prayer team member(s) in your group of four. One of the experienced members will "captain" the time; the others will serve as "listeners." Depending on the time available, one or two people in the group will receive prayer for a core stronghold that is opposing them from walking in God's original design.

Before you begin your prayer session, remember to:

- Prepare the ministry team spiritually.
- Seal off the room and the session in prayer, taking authority over any perceived or potential activity of the enemy and inviting the presence of the Holy Spirit.
- Greet and prepare your prayer candidate.

(Refer to the "Praying for Original Design" exercise, pages 21-23, if review is needed on the above procedure)

The captain will inquire of the Lord using following questions:

"Lord, what core stronghold do you wish to deal with in this person's life today?"

"How does this stronghold practically play out in this person's life/ what does it look like?"

The prayer team should listen to the Holy Spirit and write down on their notepads what they receive. This may be in the form of words, phrases, mental pictures, and/or Scriptures. Each listener should pass his or her notes to the captain, who can choose ONE core stronghold to deal with during this session. If there are several completely different issues, the captain should determine which one to address. Ask the two questions separately, asking the second question AFTER the captain has determined which core stronghold should be addressed in the prayer time.

© 2024 SycPub Global, LLC. All Rights Reserved. Do not reprint without prior written permission.

The captain should offer the revelation to the person receiving prayer. If the candidate sees it and recognizes it, the captain should proceed to lead him or her in applying the 4R prayer model. If the person finds the issue difficult to recognize, the captain can ask the Holy Spirit for further clarification and more words or pictures about what it looks like in terms of behavior or thought patterns.

If the prayer candidate does not resonate with the particular issue raised by the team, the prayer team captain should choose another that was received in prayer by the team, and see if that one is more readily recognizable to the candidate.

Lead the person in praying through the 4Rs regarding the stronghold and the ways it plays out in the candidate's life. The 4R prayer model, as learned in the *Living Set Free* course, will be addressed in more detail in our next teaching session, but for now it is sufficient to just address each point simply:

- **Repent** of the sin or lie believed.
- **Rebuke** the enemy's influence in and through the sin or the lie believed.
- **Replace** the lies and sin with the truth and right actions.
- **Receive** God's forgiveness and the indwelling power of the Holy Spirit.

Pray a prayer of blessing and impartation over the person receiving prayer, praying in scriptural truth and components of godly character and/or his (or her) original design that are opposite to the stronghold/lie just addressed in prayer.

THE FOLLOW-UP

Debrief and discuss with the group:
- How did the person receiving prayer find the exercise?
- How did those who prayed/listened find the exercise?
- Were there things that were not clear?
- Are there any questions?

NOTE: The total time of prayer for each person should not take more than 30-40 minutes so that there is also time for 20-30 minutes of discussion and debriefing afterwards.

AT-HOME ASSIGNMENT

1. As recommended in the last session, re-read this session after having prayed with your team and the prayer candidate regarding one core stronghold. Note any thoughts, impressions, or questions that come up in your mind as you do so.

2. Prepare for the next session of your training by reading Session Three: Breaking into Freedom Strongholds and the "4Rs."

3. In the *Walking in Freedom* manual or the *Living Set Free Course Manual* Resource Section, personally work through the sections assigned by your instructor.

4. Choose one or two items to pray through for yourself as the Holy Spirit leads. Be mindful: What is the Lord saying to you about *you*?

{ SESSION THREE }
BREAKING INTO FREEDOM
STRONGHOLDS AND THE "4Rs"

If you abide in My Word and My Word abides in you, then you shall know the truth and the truth shall make you free...
John 8:32 (NLT)

It was for freedom that Christ set us free...
For you were called to freedom...
Galatians 5:1, 13 (NLT)

An early Church father, Saint Irenaeus, said, "The glory of God is man truly alive."[1] Many times, however, we feel anything but fully alive. Our "glory"—all that is God in us—often feels hidden, as if with a veil. Even those whom we might consider giants of the faith felt this way: Moses said he couldn't speak (Ex. 4:10), Gideon said his clan was the weakest and he was the least in his family (Jud. 6:14), and David was just a shepherd boy in the fields (1 Sam. 16:11-12).

As believing followers of Jesus and those who have been commissioned to advance His ministry and Kingdom on earth, we must dare to look under what some have called the "delusion of ordinariness."[2] We need to see our true selves and experience the glory of God demonstrated in us. This is a significant part of what Jesus came to do for us. He is in the business of restoring what was lost and bringing us back to our original design in Him, including the full glory of all He intends for our lives.

Essentially, that is the goal of freedom prayer ministry: to help people peel back the lies, wounds, injustices, bondages, and obstructions of the enemy that have veiled and corrupted God's design for their lives.

Freedom prayer is NOT a counseling model. It is a biblical process for helping people appropriate the power of the cross and resurrection of Jesus Christ over sin and Satan.

This process involves distinct spiritual principles of repentance, receiving and granting forgiveness, resisting and rebuking the minions of Satan's kingdom, making declarations of applying truth in one's life, and praying to receive an infilling of God's Holy Spirit to live the God-empowered life. In this session we will look at each of these spiritual principles in turn.

BASIC PROCESS OF FREEDOM PRAYER MINISTRY

Freedom prayer seeks to identify and dismantle the obstructions that hold a person back from:

- living fully in his or her original design
- hindering him/her from living in obedience to and right relationship with God
- experiencing emotional (and sometimes physical) health
- enjoying peaceful, harmonious relationships
- being formed into the image of Christ through ongoing sanctification
- hearing God's voice clearly

These obstructions will many times be strongholds—entrenched and recurring sin patterns in attitude, thought, or action that have given a rightful place to the enemy's kingdom in people's lives. These strongholds may be a person's sinful reactions to things that have happened to him or her such as injustices, love deficits, or trauma. There may be other ways in which the enemy's kingdom has gained access such as generational strongholds or occult activities. We can identify these strongholds and access points through observation and also through hearing God's voice in prophetic prayer.

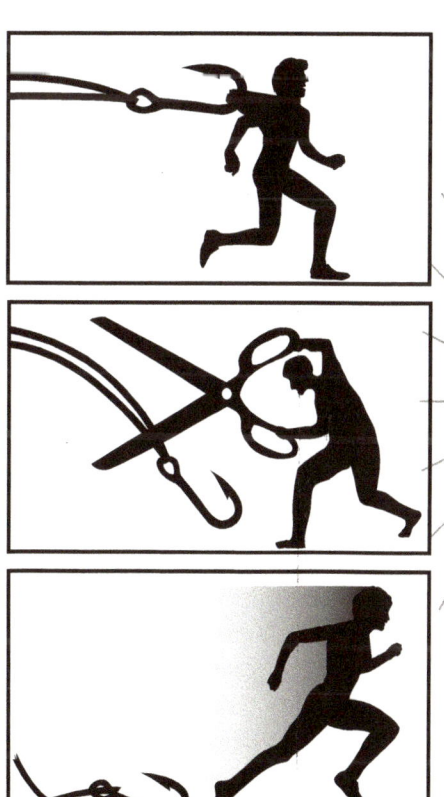
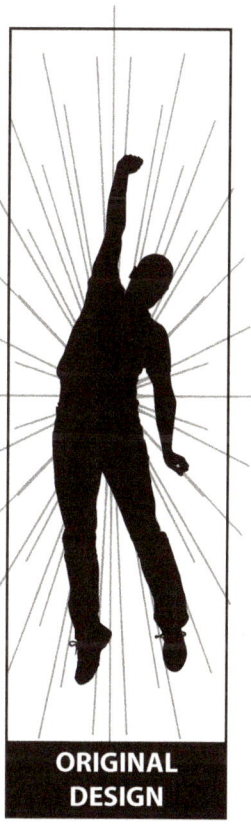

ORIGINAL DESIGN

In order to remove the barriers to someone walking fully in his original design and growing into the image of Jesus Christ, a person needs to remove the jurisdiction/right the enemy has in his life. This happens by:

- taking responsibility for and repenting of his own sin/strongholds and how they play out in his life presently

Notes:

- granting forgiveness where necessary regarding the "roots" in the past
- rebuking any evil spirits associated with those strongholds
- declaring a replacement with truth into his life
- receiving the infilling of God's spirit in order to live in God's power in the future

A person then actively needs to choose to walk in the opposite spirit of the sin and strongholds that have been identified, seeking to live out his original design in God's power and freedom, alert to the enemy's schemes in the areas he has dealt with.

STRONGHOLDS: A REVIEW OF HOW THEY ARE BUILT

Before helping people identify and dismantle strongholds in their lives, it is important that we have a clear understanding of how those strongholds are established and maintained. Please review the basic teaching on strongholds in the *Living Set Free* manual and book (see Sections 4-5 in the *Living Set Free Course Manual* and Chapters 10-14 in *Living Set Free: Recovering God's Original Design for Your Life*).

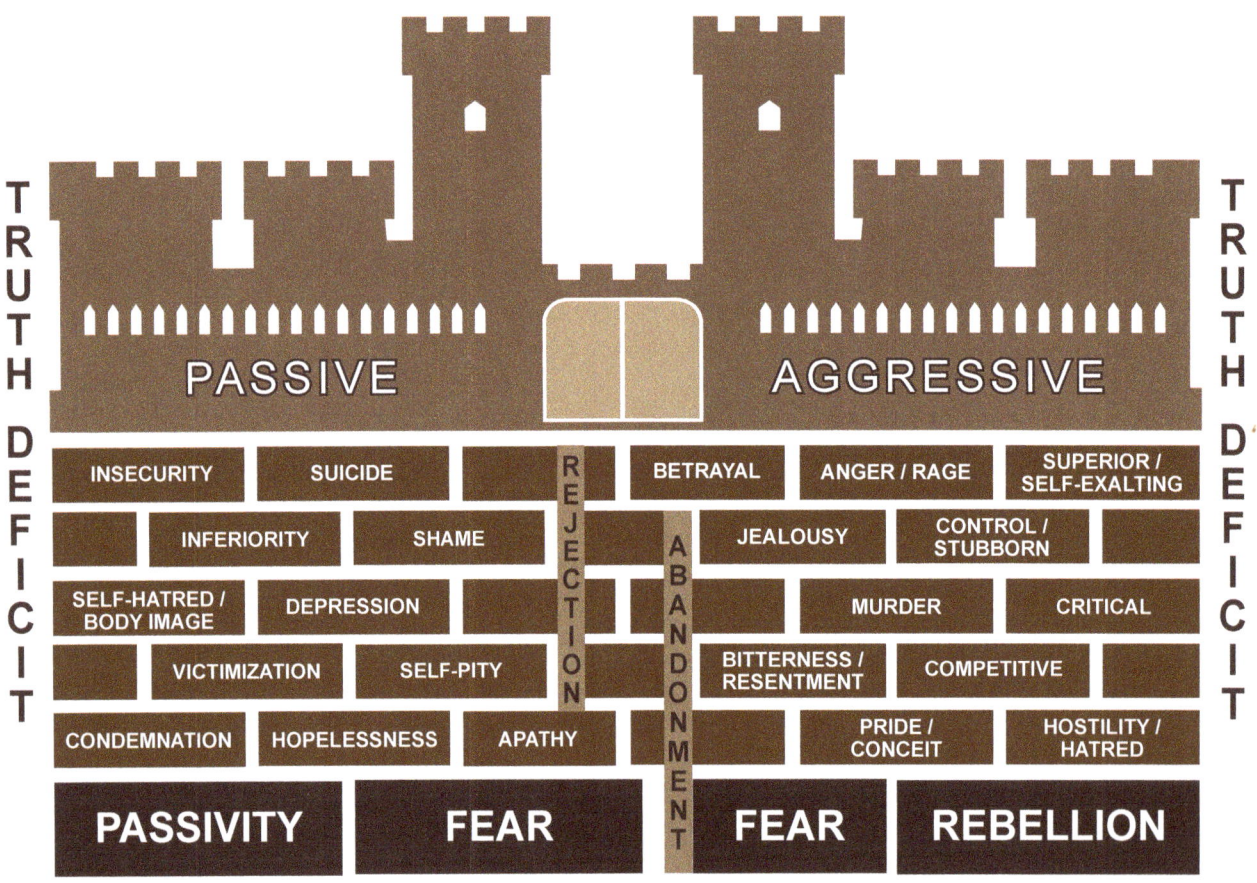

Basically, strongholds are thoughts, attitudes, or mindsets that are not in alignment with God's truth and that, left unchecked, develop into pervading mindsets or behavior patterns. The concept of a stronghold can be compared to a fortified fortress or military base of operations. The New American Standard Bible translates this concept as "fortresses" of wrong thinking:

2 Corinthians 10:3-5 (NASB)
For though we walk in the flesh, we do not war according to the flesh, for the weapons of our warfare are not of the flesh, but divinely powerful for the destruction of fortresses. We are destroying speculations and every lofty thing raised up against the knowledge of God, and we are taking every thought captive to the obedience of Christ.

> Strongholds are thoughts, attitudes, or mindsets not in alignment with God's truth and that, left unchecked, develop into pervading mindsets or behavior patterns.

As taught in *Living Set Free*, another word that helps us understand strongholds is the Greek word *topos*, which is generally translated "place," "opportunity," or "foothold." When people continue without repentance in attitudes, thoughts, or mindsets that are against the truth of God, this gives way to actions of sin that provide permission for the enemy's kingdom to have a "place" or *topos* in their lives.

Ephesians 4:26-27 (NKJV)
Be angry, and do not sin: do not let the sun go down on your wrath, nor give place to the devil.

The building of a stronghold starts in the mind with wrong thinking, believing lies about ourselves and/or about God. Then those thoughts become decisions, the decisions lead to actions, and the actions lead us into a lifestyle that is out of alignment with God's truth.

It is important to recognize (especially as prayer teams guarding our vocabulary when we communicate to prayer candidates) that the enemy cannot "take possession" of a believer. Human beings are comprised of three parts: our body, our soul (mind, emotions, and will) and our spirit (God consciousness). Once a person gives his life to Christ, his spirit is made alive and is secured in Jesus Christ. He can only be *possessed* by the Holy Spirit.

Christians certainly can be *influenced* by Satan's kingdom and by demonic spirits, however. The human soul is the primary target of the enemy in establishing strongholds. Our mind, emotions, and will can be compromised by the enemy's kingdom and influence. Our bodies are also vulnerable to attack from the enemy. This is an arena in which freedom prayer ministry can bring real relief and deliverance.

IDENTIFYING AND DISMANTLING STRONGHOLDS THROUGH FREEDOM PRAYER

In the next two sections we will look at how we can help people identify and dismantle strongholds through freedom prayer, both in terms of cultivating the heart attitude needed and in taking practical steps in using divinely powerful weapons to pull down strongholds in our lives.

HUMILITY AND A "SHAME-FREE ZONE"

The road of freedom begins with the disposition of humility. Humility confesses, "I don't have it all together." It is seeing my sin as God sees it. It confesses that I need help from God and others. It enables me to receive admonishment and correction from the Lord and others.

This mindset among a community of believers creates a shame-free zone! It empowers each and every person to embark on a road of confession and repentance, in which the destination is freedom, rejoicing, living in a greater release of God's presence and power, and the fruit of His righteousness.

As we see each other through God's eyes, seeing the potential in each of us to live according to our original design, this also helps to reinforce this "shame-free zone" in our freedom prayer times, families, small groups, and our churches as a whole.

THE "4R'S"

In freedom prayer, prayer teams help people take hold of divinely powerful weapons God has given us in Christ. These include repentance, taking authority over the enemy's schemes, standing in God's truth, and receiving the empowering work of the Holy Spirit in our lives.

These are the tools God has given to bring spiritual transaction. It is a participation in the "human-divine cooperative," in which God will do what only He can do when we do what God has asked us to do. The primary focus in this interaction is truth rather than emotions. Once we have dealt with the offending or opposing issues in prayer, according to God's prescription (repenting of wrong attitudes, taking authority over the enemy's schemes and replacing lies with God's truth), then the emotions can follow and come into alignment.

As we have grown in understanding and application of these truths and divinely powerful weapons, we have found it helpful to put the practical steps into an easily memorable outline of four steps, all beginning with the letter "R." This is not a magic formula; it is simply a helpful outline to help people easily remember the principles and keep track of progress during prayer times:

Freedom prayer is NOT a counseling model. It is a biblical process for helping people appropriate the power of the cross and resurrection of Jesus Christ over sin and Satan.

REPENT
Repentance is recognizing and turning from our own strongholds and sinful activity, removing the "place" or *topos* the enemy has in our lives. True repentance is more than mere prayer. However, the confession of sin and making a commitment to full repentance in prayer is a critical first step in the repentance process.

This step not only includes asking forgiveness but also granting forgiveness as necessary. Unforgiveness is a sin that will bind and cripple people, and impede the freedom process.

REBUKE
Taking up the authority we have in Jesus, we rebuke any influence of the enemy from our lives, commanding any evil spirits related to the strongholds to be gone.

REPLACE
We replace the stronghold and lies with God's truth, making a verbal declaration to walk in the opposite spirit (and then doing it).

RECEIVE
We receive the empowering of the Holy Spirit to enable us to walk in God's truth.

THE 4R'S IN FREEDOM PRAYER

RE-THINKING REPENTANCE

Most prayer candidates will need to take a fresh look at repentance because they come into the prayer time with a negative impression of what "repentance" actually is. In freedom prayer, we reclaim the biblical truth about repentance as a gift from God, a gateway to freedom, and a release from the power and condemnation of sin. Scripture tells us that it is God's kindness that brings us to repentance (Rom. 2:4).

Repentance leads to "times of refreshing" (Acts 3:19). It is a powerful weapon! Our goal as prayer teams is to help our candidates boldly take hold of it and appropriate it as the gift it is.

Acts 3:19 (NLT)
Repent, then, and turn to God, so that your sins may be wiped out, that times of refreshing may come from the Lord.

True Repentance

As taught in the *Living Set Free* course, an irreducible definition of repentance would be from the Greek word *metanoia*, which simply means "to change one's mind." In reality, it is more profound and comprehensive than a change of mind; it is in fact a change of life direction. In fact, John the Baptist directly *commanded* his listeners to prove by the way they live that they had repented of their sins and turned to God (Lk. 3:8). In freedom prayer ministry, we also take this view of Biblical repentance, which practically includes:

- identification and recognition of the sin and acknowledgment that it is wrong before God
- a level of sorrow or appreciation for how the sin grieves God
- confession of it as sin, asking God's forgiveness, and then, in faith, receiving God's forgiveness
    - a declaration to stop believing the lie or living out the sin, and a volitional decision to renounce/reject the sin and live obediently in the opposite direction.

The Difference Between Condemnation and Conviction

An emphasis on repentance should not be confused with condemnation. When some people hear the word "repentance" they can slip into wallowing in self-condemnation. This is not God's intention for us; we know that there is NO condemnation for those who are in Christ Jesus (Rom. 8:1).

Condemnation is from the enemy and makes people want to hide from God. It feels heavy and makes them want to stay in that place of hiddenness and isolation. Conviction, on the other hand, is from the Holy Spirit and is very different. It draws us to God so that we can deal with the sin quickly. It is a gateway to freedom and life.

Be careful that what you present is not misheard or misunderstood as condemnation. The Holy Spirit does bring conviction of sin; however, it does not have to be heavy and drawn out. It should simply move people swiftly to repentance, which is a gift of God to bring them to freedom.

2 Corinthians 7:9-10 (NIV)
Yet now I am happy, not because you were made sorry, but because your sorrow led you to repentance. For you

became sorrowful as God intended and so were not harmed in any way by us. Godly sorrow brings repentance that leads to salvation and leaves no regret, but worldly sorrow brings death.

Conscious Receiving of Forgiveness

It is important that we encourage those we pray with to take a moment to consciously receive the forgiveness of God once they have repented. Skipping over this can leave people in feelings of condemnation, unsure of whether they have repented sufficiently for God to forgive them.

Sample repentance prayer:

Dear Heavenly Father, I recognize, identify, and confess my sin of _____. I recognize that it has grieved You and I am sorry. I ask forgiveness for every way it has affected my relationship with You and others. I ask forgiveness for how it specifically has been expressed in my life. I ask forgiveness for how I have demonstrated it in my words or actions of _____ (be specific). In repentance I commit to breaking this sin pattern of _____ in my life and walking in the opposite direction through my thoughts and actions. (A similar prayer would be prayed for every sin and expression of the sin.)

Father, I receive Your forgiveness and thank You that You forgive me freely and completely.

CONDEMNATION:
- Is from the enemy
- Is heavy
- Is protracted
- Makes us hide from God
- Direction of movement is away from God

CONVICTION:
- Is from the Holy Spirit
- Swiftly moves us to repentance and freedom
- Direction of movement is towards God

Granting Forgiveness and Making Restitution

In some cases, at this first step of repentance, prayer will need to include granting forgiveness to someone who has deeply wounded the prayer candidate. This is essential in relinquishing all territory of the enemy related to that stronghold and MUST be done in order for the person to move forward in freedom. Encourage the prayer candidate to forgive out of obedience to God and resistance to the enemy, even if he or she does not "feel" like it.

The captain can make a note during the prayer time of the situations or individuals toward which the candidate needs to extend forgiveness, making a list down the side of his or her notepad.

Also, if the prayer candidate's own actions or attitudes have brought harm, injury, loss, or offense to others, he should declare how he will make it right. This is called "restitution," and is often an essential step in the process of breaking free from the enemy's influence (and sometimes outright bondage). Many times, without this important step, people continue to hang on to feelings of shame, guilt, and regret which the enemy energizes against them. There can also be hindered relationships between people until people acknowledge their own offenses, ask for forgiveness, and make right the wrong they committed to the best of their ability. We see this principle in the biblical account of Zaccheus, who gave back to the poor all that he had stolen and more after his transformational encounter with Jesus (Lk. 19:1-10).

Sample prayer for extending forgiveness and making restitution:

Dear Heavenly Father, I now grant forgiveness to _____ for the injustice or offense of _____ I received from him/her/them. I acknowledge that the actions and/or words of injustice made me feel _____. (NOTE: It is important for the person to identify and express the feelings or effects of the injustice or offense.) *As You have forgiven me I forgive them. I release them totally and fully as You have released me from the debt of my sin toward You. I now speak and pray blessing over _____.*

(NOTE: The person should speak specific blessings over the life of the person.)

And Lord, for the ways that I have brought offense, harm, or wounding to _____ (name specifically) by my attitudes, actions, or neglect, I make the determination to make restitution by (specifically name action to be taken). I will humbly apologize and seek forgiveness as You lead and as is appropriate to the situation, and do everything I can, so far as it lies with me, to make things right.

> It is important that we encourage those we pray with to take a moment to consciously receive the forgiveness of God once they have repented. Skipping over this can leave people in feelings of condemnation, unsure of whether they have repented sufficiently for God to forgive them.

REBUKING THE ENEMY

REBUKE

As believers we are raised up with Christ (Eph. 2:4-6), and in that position have authority to "overcome all the power of the enemy" (Lk. 10:17-19). Amazingly, the very power that raised Jesus from the dead is the same power that is at work in us (Eph. 1:19-22). This power and authority was not just given to Jesus' initial disciples but to all who believe (Jn. 14:12). In freedom prayer ministry, you are helping people wake up to the power and authority they have in Christ, so they do not simply lie down and let the enemy rob and steal from their lives and families.

The Apostle James tells us to "resist the devil and he will flee" (Jas. 4:7). We help our prayer candidate do this by exhorting him/her to exercise Jesus Christ's authority, which he/she has by being in right relationship with Him in salvation.

In this second step of freedom prayer, you will help the prayer candidate rebuke the enemy's influence related to the stronghold(s) in his (or her) life, commanding any evil spirit related to that stronghold (for example, the spirit of fear) to leave.

This aspect of the prayer time cannot be minimized. Many Westernized Christians do not recognize how significant this part of the spiritual transaction really is. As we learned in the *Living Set Free* course, demonic activity is very active against our lives and is closely connected to sin and strongholds.

Ephesians 6:12 (NLT)
For we are not fighting against flesh-and-blood enemies, but against evil rulers and authorities of the unseen world, against mighty powers in this dark world, and against evil spirits in the heavenly places.

RENOUNCE

Besides ensuring that prayer candidates rebuke specific demonic influence(s), you will help them renounce the lies they have believed that gave a place to that influence to begin with. To renounce means "to give up, refuse, or resign usually by formal declaration; to refuse to follow, obey, or recognize any further."[3] As people rebuke the influence of the enemy in their lives, they also

> To renounce means "to give up, refuse, or resign usually by formal declaration; to refuse to follow, obey, or recognize any further.

need to refuse/renounce any specific lies they have believed about themselves, God, or others—lies that have been the foundations of the exposed stronghold. Renouncing is simply a declaration that the prayer candidates are refusing to follow, obey, or recognize that influence in their lives any more.

Sample prayer for rebuking the enemy/renouncing lies believed:

In the authority and power of Jesus Christ that is mine in my union with Him, I resist and rebuke every spirit of __(related to the sin that has been confessed, e.g., fear)__. I command you to go the feet of Jesus. I have confessed and repented of this sin and stronghold and you no longer have any rightful place in my life. I declare myself released and freed from your activity.

I expose and renounce the lies of _____ and declare that I will no longer live my life according to these lies but according to God's truth.

Replacing sin/lies with the opposite spirit and righteous action

Replacing the lies of the strongholds with specific biblical truth and replacing sin with specific acts of righteousness—choosing to walk in the opposite direction to our sin—are absolutely critical in the process. Jesus declared that if one does not fill up the emptied house with righteousness, a delivered person will end up in a dramatically worse state than before (Mt. 12:43-45).

REPLACING LIES WITH TRUTH

At this point you can help the prayer candidate identify specific truth(s) that will replace the lie(s) of the identified stronghold. The prayer team captain may ask the listeners to spend time listening to the Holy Spirit for these specific truths and Scriptures while the captain leads the person in prayers of repentance and rebuking/renouncing. You can then encourage the person to declare these truths aloud.

Romans 12:2 (NLT)
Do not conform any longer to the pattern of this world, but be transformed by the renewing of your mind. Then you will be able to test and approve what God's will is—his good, pleasing and perfect will.

For example, someone who has dealt with the stronghold of fear might claim the following truths:

- I can trust in God.
- Perfect love casts out fear—God's love for me is perfect so I do not need to fear (1 Jn. 4:18).

- "God alone is my rock and my salvation; he is my fortress, I shall never be shaken…Find rest, O my soul, in God alone; my hope comes from him. Trust in him at all times; pour out your hearts to him, for God is our refuge" (Ps. 62:2, 5, 8).

If your prayer candidate has believed lies of insignificance, that she is unlovable or unimportant, she can claim the truth that she is of high importance to God, precious in His eyes and fearfully and wonderfully made by Him (Ps. 139:13-14). She can declare that God has engraved her on the palms of His hands (Is. 49:16). The prayer team can help by offering specific Scriptures that illustrate and emphasize the truths relevant to each specific prayer time.

The captain or a listener should write down these truths and Scriptures to give to the prayer candidate to take home so he or she can focus on them, meditate on them, and continue to claim them. You may even encourage your candidate to write a few of the truths and Scriptures on a piece of paper and put it where it can be seen often.

Replacing sin with righteous living

When Jesus told His disciples they would know the truth and the truth would set them free (Jn. 8:32), He was speaking of an experiential knowledge of truth, a truth evidenced in the way they lived their lives.

As well as helping your prayer candidate replace lies with truth, you likewise need to help him identify specific attitudes and actions that must now occupy his (or her) life so as to actively replace the recognized and confessed sin. Again, the listeners might be asked to spend time listening for this "strategy" (or action steps) while the captain leads the person through prayer.

For example, if someone has been dealing with the strongholds of insignificance and fear of man, which has led to a behavior pattern of drinking too much, he needs to consciously decide to amend this behavior and follow through with it. If someone has been dealing with a stronghold of fear and control, lacking trust in God and other people, he will need to consciously commit to surrendering to God's control in each specific area of life, without orchestrating situations personally.

These must be declared with conviction and integrity. This is the fullness of repentance. Without such life action, repentance has not taken place.

Ephesians 4:22-24 (NLT)
You were taught, with regard to your former way of life, to put off your old self, which is being corrupted by its deceitful desires; to be made new in the attitude of your minds; and to put on the new self, created to be like God in true righteousness and holiness.

Sample replacement prayer:

I declare that I will renew my thinking, replacing the lies with the specific truth of _____ regarding myself, God, and others. I declare that by the power of God's Spirit and grace, I will exercise myself to replace the sin of _____(recognized and confessed sin) with the actions of _____. I will do this by _____ (identify what walking in the opposite spirit will specifically look like).

RECEIVING THE HOLY SPIRIT'S EMPOWERING

We cannot walk in God's ways in our own strength (that is striving). We need the Holy Spirit's empowering. Here you will help your prayer candidate pray for Holy Spirit filling, claim in faith the empowering and infilling work of the Holy Spirit to walk in His power and His ways. Encourage the candidate to rejoice in the abundant grace and peace that is his (or hers) in the Holy Spirit, and the work that Jesus has done and will be doing in his life!

Titus 3:4-6
But when the kindness and love of God our Savior appeared, he saved us, not because of righteous things we had done, but because of his mercy. He saved us through the washing of rebirth and renewal by the Holy Spirit, whom he poured out on us generously through Jesus Christ our Savior.

Ephesians 5:18
. . . be filled with the Spirit.

Sample prayer for receiving God's forgiveness and the Holy Spirit's power:

I have received Your forgiveness, Lord. I now pray that You will fill me with Your Holy Spirit in a fresh way and in a fresh measure to live out my life in obedience to You and triumphant over the enemy in supernatural power. Thank You for Your Holy Spirit. Thank You that You delight to answer such prayers. I walk in the confidence that You have answered and will be answering this prayer.

Point out to your prayer candidate that he is not pleading with God to forgive and hoping He might if he repents right and is sorry enough, or if God is in a good mood. When we repent, God is faithful and just and will forgive us our sins (1 Jn. 1:9). He forgives immediately, wholeheartedly and completely—not begrudgingly as if we need to persuade Him to do so (Ps. 103:8-12). He is like the father in the story of the Prodigal Son, running to meet us and welcome us back (Lk. 15).

1 John 1:8-10 (NIV)
If we confess our sins, he is faithful and just and will forgive us our sins and purify us from all unrighteousness.

Psalm 103:8-12 (NIV)
The LORD is compassionate and gracious, slow to anger, abounding in love. He will not always accuse, nor will he harbor his anger forever; he does not treat us as our sins deserve or repay us according to our iniquities. For as high as the heavens are above the earth, so great is his love for those who fear him; as far as the east is from the west, so far has he removed our transgressions from us.

PRACTICAL EXERCISE: Praying through Passivity

God's design and purpose for a person is viciously opposed by sin, strongholds, and the schemes of Satan's dark kingdom. True freedom and sanctification come as believers identify besetting sins and strongholds, and exercise the divinely powerful weapons that God has given His believing followers.

In our practical exercise for this session we will pray for one another regarding the stronghold issue of passivity. You will work again with an experienced prayer team minister(s). One of the experienced members will captain the time while you and the others serve as listeners.

Depending on the time available, one or two people in the group will receive prayer concerning how passivity is opposing him/her/them from walking in God's original design and truth. Before you begin your prayer session, remember to:

1. Prepare the ministry team spiritually.

2. Seal off the room and the session in prayer, taking authority over any perceived or potential activity of the enemy and inviting the presence of the Holy Spirit.

3. Greet and prepare your prayer candidate.

(Refer to the "Praying for Original Design" exercise, pages 21-23, if review is needed on the above procedure.)

The captain will inquire of the Lord using the following question:

"How does passivity practically play out in this person's life/what does it look like?"

The prayer team should listen to the Holy Spirit and write down on their notepads what they receive. This may be in the form of words, phrases, mental pictures, and/or Scriptures. Each listener should pass his or her notes to the captain, who can choose what to present to the candidate.

If there are several completely different issues, the captain should determine which one to address. Ask the two questions separately, asking the second question AFTER the captain has determined which core stronghold should be addressed in the prayer time.

The captain should offer the revelation to the prayer candidate. If the candidate sees it and recognizes it, the captain should proceed to lead him or her in prayer. **Use the 4R prayer model as described in detail in this lesson, this time being sure to include the critical component of extending forgiveness and restitution where necessary.**

Repent of the area of passivity and how it has played out.

Rebuke the enemy's influence in and through it.

Replace the lies and sin with the truth and right actions, extending forgiveness to offenders and determining to seek forgiveness/make restitution for one's own attitudes/actions/neglect.

Receive God's forgiveness and the indwelling power of the Holy Spirit.

Finally, **pray a prayer of blessing and impartation** over the person receiving prayer. Bless him and pray in Scriptural truth and components of godly character and/or his original design that are opposite to the stronghold/lies just addressed in prayer.

THE FOLLOW-UP

Debrief and discuss with the group:
- How did the person receiving prayer find the exercise?
- How did those on the training course who prayed/listened find the exercise?
- Did things go any differently than last week? How?
- Were there things that were not clear?
- Are there any questions?

The total time of prayer for each person should not take more than 30-40 minutes, so that there is also time for 20-30 minutes to discuss and debrief afterwards.

AT-HOME ASSIGNMENT

1. Thoroughly re-read this session after having prayed with your team and the prayer candidate regarding passivity. Make notes in the margins on points you want to review or emphasize for next time, or about questions you'd like to ask.

2. Read the next session (Session Four: Walking through a Freedom Prayer Session), before the next class.

3. Review the sections in SycPub Global's *Walking in Freedom* manual or *Living Set Free Course Manual* as assigned by your instructor. Continue to familiarize yourself with the concepts and vocabulary related to the various stronghold issues listed in the manual and commonly encountered in freedom prayer ministry.

4. As you read, continue to ask the Holy Spirit what He wants to say to you about *you*. Use the 4R prayer model to pray through any issues you encounter in your studies that the Holy Spirit highlights to you, personally.

{ SESSION FOUR }
RECEIVING AND HANDLING REVELATION

"Follow the way of love and eagerly desire spiritual gifts, especially the gift of prophecy."
1 Corinthians 14:1 (NLT)

Of all the essential biblical truths covered (and needed) in this course, this session's topic—that of receiving and handling revelation from the Holy Spirit—is probably the most foundational and the most opposed. That's because the devil seems to work overtime convincing God's children that they don't hear, can't hear, and shouldn't hear the voice of the Spirit. Or, when they do, the seed is stolen and carried away by doubt, fear, unbelief, misinterpretation, or just plain "weirdness."

It doesn't have to be that difficult!

There is a very simple and yet important principle in helping to protect the accuracy and credibility of hearing God's voice and of prophetic ministry in particular. It is crucial to understand and keep distinct these separate components to hearing God's voice. These components can be separated into the following three distinct functions:

1. **REVELATION**
2. **INTERPRETATION**
3. **APPLICATION**

(These concepts are taught more thoroughly in Sycamore Publications' course and manual, *Hearing God's Voice for Yourself and Others* by Mike Riches and Tom Jonez. We have adapted that material here for freedom prayer training purposes, but please take time to go back to that manual and review.)

Notes:

Confusion and misunderstandings as to exactly what the Lord is communicating can occur if we do not understand the importance of differentiating between revelation, interpretation, and application. This can also result in confusion and pain for other people involved. By misunderstanding or neglecting these three distinctions, people can readily jump to unwarranted conclusions.

REVELATION

When the Lord communicates indirectly or cryptically, we must treat each component distinctly by seeking God's mind on each component, having first prepared ourselves personally. This includes repenting of any known sin the Holy Spirit brings to our mind. This is important, as Scripture reminds us through the Psalmist David, "If I had cherished sin in my heart, the Lord would not have listened" (Ps. 66:18).

God-given revelation in a prayer session may come in a number of ways, and we need to learn to be alert to all of them. Some examples include (but are not limited to):

- Scripture or a word from a Scripture
- biblical character representing a particular character quality, sin pattern, or attitude
- mental picture
- a single word or phrase
- a thought, feeling, or impression
- a physical sensation

INTERPRETATION

After we receive what we believe by faith to be His revelation, we move to the next step: seeking interpretation. The initial process is the same as above. Having prepared ourselves, we ask the Lord by faith for His help in interpreting what we received. We have faith in our God and we believe He is able to grant us interpretation, just as Joseph reminded Pharaoh in their famous exchange:

Genesis 41:15-16 (NLT)
Pharaoh said to Joseph, "I had a dream, and no one can interpret it. But I have heard it said of you that when you hear a dream you can interpret it." "I cannot do it," Joseph replied to Pharaoh, "but God will give Pharaoh the answer he desires" (emphasis added).

Since interpretation can be somewhat new to people, we want to be clear that there is in fact a helpful hint: The key is to ask the Lord questions! It is not, as Joseph readily admitted to Pharaoh, our own human ability that makes the difference when it comes to interpretation. Rather, thankfully, it is the Lord's ability to answer the questions we are asking that gives us confidence when we ask. If we need clarity at this point, the captain can ask in prayer, *"What does this [symbol, picture, number] mean and how does it apply to this [person, situation]?"*

Humility—in the specific form of admitting we don't know and simply asking the Lord our specific and diagnostic questions—is actually a great asset in interpretation.

On a practical note, if you receive revelation for another person, it is your responsibility to offer it in humility for consideration to the recipient, not to interpret it in absolute terms or to tell him or her what to do to act on it. If the person requests assistance with interpretation, you can proceed to offer assistance. Regardless, the key is to operate with an acute sense of humility and to avoid at all costs any hint of manipulation or control.

APPLICATION

This is the step the candidate must take to apply what was received to his or her own situation. This is also the step where it's possible, if we're not careful, to overstep our boundaries. Remember that freedom prayer ministry is not a counseling model. We are not there to give the candidates advice or direction for their lives. We are there to help them hear the voice of the Holy Spirit for them, and to offer support and agreement in prayer. Therefore, at this juncture, it is important to help the candidate identify what the application steps might be without telling him or her what to do.

We will find that seldom is the *revelation* wrong. Difficulties and confusion usually occur when people do not give due diligence to the interpretation and application steps. We therefore strongly encourage people to not jump to conclusions without first considering each step in the process described above. If you take these precautions, you will no doubt find confusion and misunderstandings minimized.

HOW TO PRESENT WHAT YOU RECEIVE

When we present insight received in prayer from the Lord concerning the roots of people's strongholds, we are often dealing with the very most sensitive parts of people's lives and emotions. Additionally, we are dealing with spiritual strongholds that have been in—in the heavenlies realm—legitimate jurisdiction or *topos* of the enemy.

With that in mind, always be sensitive and discerning. Don't be the classic "bull in a china shop." There are sensitive ways to present what you receive—even though it may appear initially negative.

> ### PRINCIPLES FOR RECEIVING AND HANDLING HOLY SPIRIT REVELATION
>
> * Offer revelation; don't impose it
> * Use questions
> * Share what you receive without fear
> * Use appropriate boundaries
> * Use simple language and explain any jargon
> * Be realistic about time.

OFFER REVELATION; DON'T IMPOSE IT

You might say, "This is what I believe I have received, how does it resonate with you?" rather than "This is what the Lord says . . ." Offer what you have received with confidence but also with genuine humility. Leave the person room to test it for himself or herself and to feel totally free to reject it if he or she feels it is not accurate or applicable. Remember, you are not the Holy Spirit! It is the Holy Spirit's role to bring revelation and conviction, not yours.

PRESENT REVELATION POSITIVELY

Present revelation in a positive and encouraging manner even when it is regarding sin or strongholds, so there is no room for condemnation. For example, if the prayer team receives that "unbelief" is a stronghold in the person's life, the captain might share that by saying, "The Lord wants you to be strengthened by faith and not crippled with unbelief," rather than saying, "The Lord says you are filled with unbelief." You are to focus on *walking* into freedom.

USE QUESTIONS

Use questions to gain permission, trust, and a platform to speak into a person's life. By using questions, you can gently offer revelation without imposing it, while at the same time helping the prayer candidate receive and recognize it.

Example:

If you receive that the Lord wants to free the person from anger and rejection from his father, and that it is a generational issue on the father's side, you **DO NOT SAY,** *"You have anger against your father because of rejection; in fact, it has been coming down your father's side of the family for generations—let's deal with it!"*

Instead, *you always gain access to the person's life and issues by asking questions* such as:

Are you aware of anger in your life?
How would you describe your relationship with your father?
Are you aware of any pattern of rejection and/or anger in your father's family?

NOTE: Sometimes you might have to keep asking other questions to help the person realize the issue(s). This is because people often learn to cope with the violations, injustices, and strongholds to such a degree that they simply become part of their lives and seem normal to them.

Always ask questions gently and openly, not in an interrogating manner. Once the person has recognized some of the elements the captain may then feel it's appropriate to offer the revelation received more directly.

SHARE WHAT YOU RECEIVE WITHOUT FEAR

Do not be held back by fear of getting it wrong. In the freedom prayer process, there are safeguards in place:

- Listeners test the revelation against the Scriptures and the character of God.
- Revelation is submitted to the captain for his or her discernment.
- Revelation is offered to people with the qualifier that they are free to accept or dismiss it as they test it.

Generally speaking, the first thing that pops into your mind is what the Holy Spirit is saying. If you mull on it or overanalyze what you receive, confusion can set in and you begin to question it, thinking *maybe that's just my own thoughts*. When you do, you allow space for doubt to creep in and may end up holding back from offering revelation that might be critical to the person's freedom. My encouragement to you is to step out in boldness to offer what you think you have received. Trust the discernment of the captain and the sovereignty of God over the prayer time.

USE APPROPRIATE BOUNDARIES

It is wise to leave prophesying on sensitive subjects to those who are mature and proven to have an extraordinary measure in prophetic gifting. Part of protecting the ministry and reputation of the prophetic ministry is being wise in what we ask the Lord to reveal and being wise in what we share, even if we feel the Lord has revealed it. This includes having a wise and realistic perception of the measure of our gifting, experience, spiritual maturity, and track record, as well as having wise boundaries.

Romans 12:3

For by the grace given me I say to every one of you: Do not think of yourself more highly than you ought, but rather think of yourself with sober judgment, in accordance with the measure of faith God has given you.

It is wise to avoid topics such as *marriages, births of children, finances, and leaving a job/community/ministry/church*. Such things generally fall into the role of pastoral leadership in a person's life. Even then, a high level of discernment is needed on the part of both the one seeking revelation and on the recipient. Such topics need to be left to those graced with a great measure of anointing regarding the prophetic, and who have both a proven track record and are well-regarded by the leadership of their church.

USE SIMPLE LANGUAGE AND EXPLAIN ANY JARGON

Avoid using jargon or overly religious terms and phrases. When people have been walking in these truths for a while, some of the phrases and words become so familiar that it's easy to forget they are not usual language for others who are new to it. Some of the words used to describe strongholds may also need a brief explanation in order for people to recognize them. The captain might need to give a brief explanation to the prayer candidate regarding some of the words and phrases used (i.e., "original design," "spiritual DNA," "insignificance," and "passivity," etc.).

BE REALISTIC ABOUT TIME

Only attempt to cover what you can respectfully and sensibly deal with in the time allotted. Sticking to time constraints is important out of respect for the person receiving prayer.

We know that God's design and purpose for a person is viciously opposed by sin, strongholds, and the schemes of Satan's dark kingdom. True freedom comes as believers identify besetting sins and strongholds, and exercise the divinely powerful weapons God has given His believing followers. One key stronghold we need to ruthlessly root out of our lives if we are to operate in peace, faith, and obedience is that of *fear*.

In our practical exercise for this session we will pray for one another regarding the specific stronghold of fear. You will now work with an experienced prayer team minister(s). There will be at least one or two experienced prayer team members in your group of four. One of the experienced members will lead the time. The others will act as listeners. One person or two people in the group will receive prayer concerning how fear may be playing out in his or her life. In the next session, another person will receive prayer regarding this topic.

CONDUCTING THE SESSION

1. **PREPARE THE TEAM AND THE SETTING**

   Before you begin your prayer session, remember to:

   a. Prepare the ministry team spiritually.
   b. Seal off the room and the session in prayer, taking authority over any perceived or potential activity of the enemy, and inviting the presence of the Holy Spirit.
   c. Greet and prepare your prayer candidate.

   (Refer to the "Praying for Original Design" exercise, pages 21-23, if review is needed on the above procedure.)

2. **INQUIRE OF THE LORD**

   The captain will inquire of the Lord for the prayer team, using the following questions:

"How does fear practically play out in this person's life? What does it look like?"

Offer the revelation to the person. If he or she sees it and receives it, proceed to the next step.

3. LEAD THE CANDIDATE IN A 4R PRAYER

If the prayer candidate sees it and receives it, allow him to explain briefly
how it relates to his life. Then proceed to lead him in a 4R prayer. Remember to lead the candidate through forgiving any offenders that have contributed to the establishment of fear in his life, using the 4R prayer outline.

CLOSING OUT THE SESSION

Pray a prayer of impartation over the person receiving prayer, blessing him or her and praying in Scriptural truth that is opposite to the stronghold or lies believed that they have addressed in this prayer session.

Make extra effort to ensure there is adequate and emphasized time for this portion of the session. Try to use the points covered in this week's teaching to enhance and improve your impartation and blessing time.

NOTE: The total time of this exercise for each person should not take more than 30 minutes.

1. As recommended in the last session, re-read this session after having prayed with your team and the prayer candidate regarding fear. Note any thoughts, impressions, or questions that come up in your mind as you do so.

2. Prepare for the next session of your training by reading ahead in Session Five: Practicum.

3. In the *Walking in Freedom* manual or *Living Set Free Course Manual,* complete the stronghold sections recommended by your instructor.

Notes:

{ SESSION FIVE }
PRACTICUM

Brothers, if someone is caught in a sin, you who are spiritual should restore him gently. But watch yourself, or you also may be tempted. Carry each other's burdens, and in this way you will fulfill the law of Christ.
Galatians 6:1-2 (NLT)

The objective of freedom prayer ministry is to appropriate biblical truths—"divinely powerful weapons" (2 Cor. 10:3-5)—to set people free from the spiritual obstacles that prevent them from fully living out God's original design for their lives.

No two freedom prayer ministry times will ever be exactly the same. People are unique. God's original design for each person is unique. And the schemes of the enemy to oppose different people's original designs are specific toward each person. For this reason, following the lead of the Holy Spirit is so important in freedom prayer ministry. We always want to be led by Him and not by a formula. At the same time, it is good to work from a foundational pattern for the sake of order and consistency.

In this session, we will spend time reviewing the principles we've been covering in this course to date, as well as in practical prayer sessions covering the issue of injustices. Use the blank sections provided to take notes, and to write down ideas or questions you would like to share with the class or instructor during the "debriefing" time at the end of your practice sessions.

Notes:

> We always want to be led by Him and not by a formula.

Notes:

The "4Rs"

1. Repent
2. Rebuke
3. Replace
4. Receive

Notes: _____

> In order to remove the barriers to someone walking fully in his original design and growing into the image of Jesus Christ, a person needs to remove the jurisdiction/right the enemy has in his life.

PRACTICAL EXERCISE: Praying through Sin Responses to Injustices and Love Deficits

The prayer time should identify not only the injustice to be forgiven, but also the person's own sinful reactions to the injustice. The prayer team captain should collect the revelation from the listeners and have clear notes for himself (or herself) of what the person has resonated and agreed with. Along with any details the prayer candidate has offered personally, these notes will be important in leading the candidate through the prayer time.

The captain can then lead the candidate through the 4R's regarding his own sin responses, encouraging him to add his own words where desired. An example of this might be, in the case of an injustice related to withholding from the candidate's father:

1. REPENT

"Lord, I repent of my own anger and resentment against my dad. I repent of the sin of insignificance, not believing the truth of what you say about me. I repent of the ways in which I have withdrawn from people to protect myself. I repent of believing the lie that I am not lovable... (add specifics received in the prayer time, including the strongholds and also the practical ways they play out in the person's life). Lord, I receive Your forgiveness and total cleansing of these sins and I thank You for Your grace and forgiveness."

2. REBUKE

"In Jesus' name and in His authority, I rebuke every spirit of anger, resentment, insignificance, and self-protection. I command you to get out of my life and go to the feet of Jesus to be destroyed. You no longer have any right to remain. In Jesus' name I break the lie that I am unlovable; it no longer has any power over me."

3. REPLACE

"I choose to replace anger and resentment with a spirit of blessing and forgiveness. I choose to replace insignificance with the truth that my Heavenly Father delights in me and I am precious and significant in His eyes. I claim the truth that I am lovable and that God loves me extravagantly and affectionately. I choose to replace self-protection with a life of

interdependence with others, vulnerability, and deep friendships."

The prayer candidate should be specific in replacing lies; for example:

- replacing the lie that "I am unlovable" with the truth that "God loves me with an abundant and extravagant love"
- replacing the lie that "God is not trustworthy" with the truth that "I can always trust in God's unfailing love: He always keeps His promises and will never fail me"

The captain can lead here by offering specific truths to replace the lies, including Scriptures. For resources, see the *Living Set Free Course Manual*: "The Christian's Birthright," "God's Love and Forgiveness," and "Walking in the Opposite Spirit."

4. RECEIVE

"Heavenly Father, please come into the places where I have been hurt and heal me. I receive Your Holy Spirit to restore me, to flood my soul and my life with Your love and peace. I receive Your power to enable me to actively walk in Your truth."

Encourage the person to think of specific ways he will actively live out the truth, walking in the opposite spirit to his previous sin reactions and/or stronghold patterns.

IMPARTATION / BLESSING

This is an essential part of the prayer time. The prayer team captain should manage the time wisely in order to leave sufficient time for it. During this component of the session, the team prays prayers of agreement, declaration, and impartation—affirming in faith that God will bring restoration of what the enemy has stolen and will even bring good from what the enemy meant for harm through the injustice suffered. During the blessing time, the prayer team gathers around the prayer candidate (who may elect to stand or remain seated, whichever is most comfortable or appropriate), placing hands on his/her back or shoulder.

Pray in agreement with the spiritual transaction that has just taken place, affirming the candidate's humility and obedience in bringing the injustice to the foot of the cross (and leaving it there). Make declarations with Scriptures and prayers about God's love and forgiveness, His healing, restorative grace and mercy, and His power to make all things new in Christ.

1. As recommended in previous sessions, re-read this session after having prayed with your team and the prayer candidate regarding injustices. Note any thoughts, impressions, or questions that come up in your mind as you do so.

2. Prepare for the next session of your training by reading Session Six: Closing out a Ministry Session.

3. In the *Walking in Freedom* manual or *Living Set Free Course Manual*, personally work through the sections recommended by your instructor.

{ SESSION SIX }
CLOSING OUT A MINISTRY SESSION

So Ananias went and found Saul. He laid his hands on him and said, "Brother Saul, the Lord Jesus, who appeared to you on the road, has sent me so that you might regain your sight and be filled with the Holy Spirit."
Acts 9:17 (NLT)

Remember that the goal of freedom prayer ministry is not repentance or deliverance, although it certainly includes these important components. The objective is to restore a person to what God intended, to bring his or her mind, heart, will, and whole life back into alignment with God's truth and love, so that he or she is released in increased power to do the works that Jesus did, and to take a full part in the mission of the Church to advance the kingdom of God in our world. FREEDOM PRAYER IS NOT AN END GOAL. It is a tool in order to help people be increasingly released in power in serving Jesus.

REPLACING LIES WITH TRUTH AND WALKING IN THE OPPOSITE SPIRIT

An essential component of closing out a freedom prayer session is ensuring people realize that "replacing" is not just a part of the prayer they say or repeat, but that it is something that should actively continue after the session. There is a danger of the 4R prayer outline becoming a formula that we use in a "religious" way, clinging to it as a method or technique that makes us feel better. In order for change to be sustained, a person leaving a prayer session must actively choose to "fill up" with truth and God's love. Where a vacuum has been left by strongholds and lies, he or she must choose to be intentional and active in living out that truth in different behaviors.

> After receiving freedom prayer, the prayer candidate must fill the vacuum of sin and lies with righteousness and truth, embracing the truth in his or her mind, heart, and will.

This is about the opposite of simply receiving ministry passively. It means choosing to walk in freedom—consciously, actively, and aggressively. It is essential that the person receiving prayer recognize his (or her) own responsibility in this.

Matthew 3:8 (NIV)
Produce fruit in keeping with repentance.

After receiving freedom prayer, the prayer candidate must fill the vacuum of sin and lies with righteousness and truth, embracing that truth in his or her mind, heart, and will. If he or she fails to follow through on this point, it can be a major reason (really, THE major reason) for not being able to sustain a lifestyle of freedom and healing. God's truth must rule in every part of our person:

- Our mind—replacing lies with Scriptural truth
- Our heart—receiving what God says over us and how He sees us
- Our wills—choosing to live differently

THE MIND

The person receiving prayer must replace with Scriptural truth the lies he or she previously believed. This is why we want to use specific truths about God's character and love and about who the person is in Christ. We want people to leave the session with their minds and hearts full of Scriptural truth about God's heart towards them. They also may need to go and search the Scriptures themselves to find truths that counter the lies they have believed.

THE HEART

The person must then replace how he used to see himself as a result of the stronghold with a picture of how God sees him in freedom from that stronghold. For example, he can consciously and intentionally replace the sense of feeling dirty and far from God with a picture of how God sees him—welcomed onto the Father's knee and given new clothes instead of rags.

This is why we ask God for prophetic pictures and words of how He sees people and what He wants to say to them in this part of the prayer session. We want people to leave the session with strong imagery of God's thoughts, truths, and character rather than their own false thinking, perceptions, and self-images.

THE EMOTIONS

Our emotions follow our minds, hearts, and wills. They are God-created. They are valid because they are a signal of what is happening in our hearts. However, they are not something we should build our lives on. As we deal with the roots of strongholds and sin patterns—replacing them with the truth—our emotions will catch up later.

We remind people who have received freedom prayer ministry not to shut out emotions but also not to let them dominate. We encourage them to beware of introspection and overanalyzing their emotions; they can be misleading. We remind them not to trust their emotions over God's word.

THE WILL

The person receiving prayer needs to actively choose to engage his or her will to make radical choices about changing behavior and living differently. Repentance isn't just for a prayer time. It requires an active walking in the opposite direction, hating the sin, and boldly making steps in the opposite direction; even if it is difficult.

A person may need to face a particular fear, step out in boldness where there has been passivity, actively trust God where there has been unbelief or fear, or submit where he has been in rebellion. If someone has struggled with isolation, he may need to initiate conversation with people. If someone is dealing with fear, he may offer to share his testimony in front of the church. If someone has been dealing with rejection, he must learn to react differently when hurts or insecurities arise. He must begin turning to God's comfort and path of blessing, forgiveness, and confidence in His love (which will require courage, faith, and obedience), rather than the old patterns of seeking false comfort in other things.

IMPARTATION AND BLESSING

God in His wisdom has chosen to do this work and ministry to humans through humans. He wants to use you and me to do His work in other's lives and to use others to do His work in our lives. We are a body. We need one another. This is a key way we serve the Lord—by serving one another.

1 Corinthians 12:12, 13, 27 (NIV)
The body is a unit, though it is made up of many parts; and though all its parts are many, they form one body. So it is with Christ. For we were all baptized by one Spirit into one body… Now you are the body of Christ, and each one of you is a part of it.

Galatians 6:1-2 (NIV)
Brothers, if someone is caught in a sin, you who are spiritual should restore him gently. But watch yourself, or you also may be tempted. Carry each other's burdens, and in this way you will fulfill the law of Christ.

One of the most strategic and powerful ways we participate in this "body life" freedom prayer ministry is in the acts of blessing and impartation. The focus in this session, as we focus on how to close out a freedom prayer ministry time, is on learning to appropriate the power that God gives us to bless each other through our words and through the laying on of hands. This part of a freedom prayer session is not just "being nice to the person so they leave feeling good." Impartation is spiritually powerful and has very real effects on a person's life.

The Example of Saul and Ananias

We see the ministry of impartation graphically demonstrated in the account of God calling and commissioning Saul of Tarsus. We are familiar with Saul's notorious reputation as an enemy of Christians. He relentlessly persecuted and martyred them. His objective was to annihilate the Church.

On Saul's travels to extend his assault against the Church in Damascus, he had an encounter with Jesus. It brought him to repentance to become a believing follower of Jesus Christ. This included hearing Jesus' audible voice speaking to him and seeing a bright light that left him blind.

God wanted to solidify Paul's conversion experience and commission him to fulfill a mission on His behalf. So He spoke to Ananias and told him to go and find Paul, lay hands on him, and to commission him.

Acts 9:17 (NIV)
So Ananias went and found Saul. He laid his hands on him and said, "Brother Saul, the Lord Jesus, who appeared to you on the road, has sent me so that you might regain your sight and be filled with the Holy Spirit."

THE ROLE OF "LAYING ON OF HANDS"

Scripture does show us, however, that it was a practice Jesus followed: *"When the sun was setting, the people brought to Jesus all who had various kinds of sickness, and laying his hands on each one, he healed them."*	(Lk. 4:40)
This was obviously not a one-time occurrence, as the Scriptures demonstrate that Jesus modeled it consistently for His disciples.	(Mt. 8:3, 17:7, 20:34; Mk. 1:41; Lk. 5:13, 22:51).
After Jesus left them with instructions to carry on His ministry (Jn. 14:12; Mt. 28:19-20; Mk. 16:15-18; Acts 1:8), the apostles and the early church continued to follow His practice of laying hands on people.	(Acts 8:18, 19:6; 1 Tim. 4:14; 2 Tim. 1:6).
The writer of Hebrews included it in a list of the elementary teachings of the Christian faith.	(Heb. 6:1-3)
Even unbelievers noted that the laying on of hands produced powerful spiritual results.	(Acts 8:18-19)

Laying hands on someone when we pray for them is not, in and of itself, particularly dramatic. Scripture refers to it simply: "When Paul placed his hands on them, the Holy Spirit came on them" (Acts 19:6). The Bible does not state specifically why we are to do it, or that it guarantees any predictable result.

In freedom prayer ministry, we follow this example when we pray for God's blessing and a Holy Spirit infilling for a prayer candidate at the end of the session. It is only through God's grace that an individual can walk out of the enemy's strongholds in freedom—and stay there. It is only by the Holy Spirit's empowering work that he can sustain that freedom by living a lifestyle of repentance and walking in the opposite spirit of his previous state. And it is in the ministry of impartation and blessing that we, as a prayer team, participate as God's vessels to impart that strength and power to our prayer candidate.

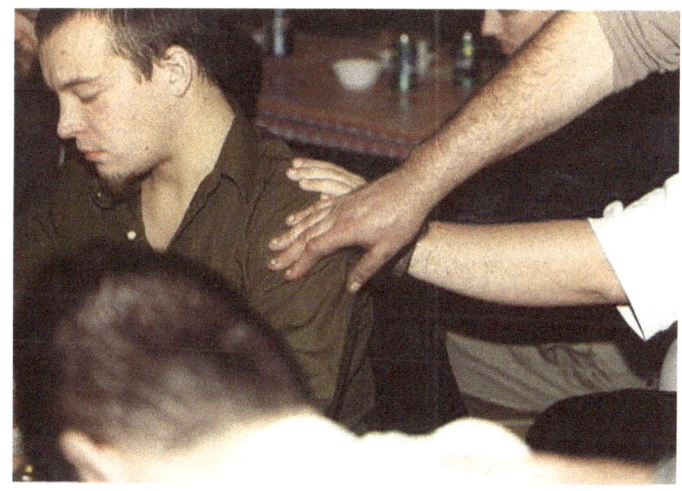

THE ROLE OF BLESSING

The Old Testament word for blessing was *berakah*, which means "a transmittal or endowment of the power of God's goodness and favor," usually through the spoken word and often with the accompanying act of the laying on of hands. In Bible times, God commanded the priests to bless the people (Num. 6:22-27).

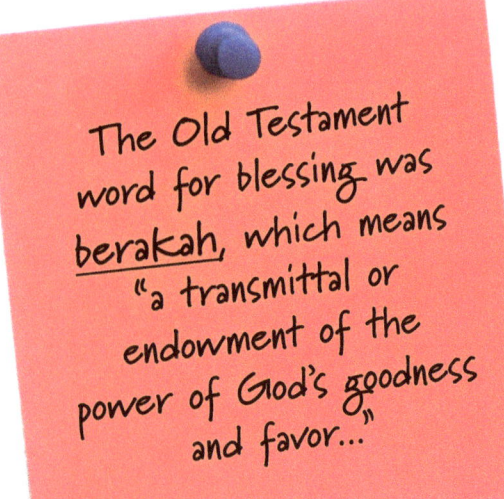

Numbers 6:22-27 (NIV)
The LORD said to Moses, "Tell Aaron and his sons, 'This is how you are to bless the Israelites. Say to them: "The LORD bless you and keep you; the LORD make his face shine upon you and be gracious to you; the LORD turn his face toward you and give you peace." ' "So they will put my name on the Israelites, and I will bless them (emphasis added)."

As New Testament believers we are all priests:

1 Peter 2:9 NIV
But you are a chosen people, a royal priesthood, a holy nation, a people belonging to God, that you may declare the praises of him who called you out of darkness into his wonderful light.

During this important component of the prayer session, we use the power of our words (Prov. 18:21) and our calling as part of the priesthood of all believers (1 Pet. 2:9) to impart God's goodness and favor to the prayer candidate. When our words are combined with God's Word in a verbal blessing, we become a channel through which God's power can flow, somewhat like a lightening rod becomes a conductor for electricity. In the same way that a lightning rod provides a path for lightning and guides it to the ground, our prayers of blessing over people can serve as points of attraction for the power of God to flow into and through their lives.

> **CLOSING OUT A TYPICAL MINISTRY SESSION**
> - ✓ Prophetically minister according to how God sees the person at this time
> - ✓ Agreement with the spiritual transaction that has just taken place
> - ✓ Affirming original design
> - ✓ Expressing God's heart and mind towards the person
> - ✓ Identifying specific replacement truths
> - ✓ Blessing
> - ✓ Impartation

CLOSING OUT A TYPICAL MINISTRY SESSION

PROPHETICALLY MINISTER ACCORDING TO HOW GOD SEES THE PERSON AT THIS TIME

Because of the huge significance of this part of the prayer session, the prayer team captain needs to manage the time wisely throughout the session in order for there to be enough time for it, and for it not to be a rushed afterthought. Essentially, the prayer team will listen to the Holy Spirit for words of blessing, encouragement, and exhortation for the prayer candidate, and will impart them to him or her through prayer and the laying on of hands.

The prayer candidate can remain seated and have the prayer team gather around him or her in a standing position. If the person is willing and able, he or she can stand and the team should stand in a circle around him or her. Asking permission first, the team can lay their hands on the shoulders, back, or arm of the person receiving prayer.

The blessing and impartation part of the prayer session should include the following components:

AGREEMENT WITH THE SPIRITUAL TRANSACTION THAT HAS JUST TAKEN PLACE

Agreement is a powerful principle in God's kingdom. Jesus said, "If two of you on earth agree about anything you ask for, it will be done for you by my Father in heaven" (Mt. 18:19). With this principle in mind, the prayer team should make declarations of agreement in prayer that might sound something like:

"Lord, we agree with the spiritual transaction that has just taken place here. We stand with our brother against the lie that _____, and in agreement with the truth that _____. We stand in agreement with him against every wicked spirit that has energized this lie (injustice, stronghold, etc.) in his life. We join him in taking authority over any such spirits in the name of Jesus Christ and by the power of His shed blood. We agree with Your design and plan for his life, Lord. He IS ___(name some specific components of the person's original design)___. We stand with him today in unity and faith to see Your Holy Spirit released in Him and for your original design and destiny to be accomplished in his life."

AFFIRMING ORIGINAL DESIGN

Ask the Holy Spirit to reveal a few aspects of God's original design for how He created the person. If the team has already listened for original design earlier in the prayer time, they can simply pray these words and pictures over the prayer candidate, affirming that this is who he truly is and how God sees him.

EXPRESSING GOD'S HEART AND MIND TOWARDS THE PERSON

Speak to the prayer candidate about God's heart, mind, and character. Affirm the reality of God's personal knowledge about, interest in, and love for him. We want to pour the truth of God's love for him into his heart. If the person has previously experienced a particular love deficit, it is good to proclaim and use Scriptures about how God's love is different and complete in every way.

IDENTIFYING SPECIFIC REPLACEMENT TRUTHS

The captain may ask the listeners to listen for specific truths, pictures, and verses that represent the opposite of the sin reactions identified (e.g., significance rather than insignificance and trust rather than fear). The team can write these down on their notepads while the captain is leading the candidate through prayer, then shared/prayed during the blessing and given to the person to keep and reflect on later.

BLESSING

During the blessing time, the prayer team makes faith-filled declarative statements in prayer over the person receiving prayer. An example of a blessing prayer might be, *"Joe, I bless you with God's strength to walk in forgiveness toward the people who have hurt you so deeply. You are a man of grace, compassion, and core inner strength that comes from a reliance on God's Holy Spirit. You have God's unconditional love deeply rooted in your heart and I bless you with an increased ability to extend that grace and love to others."* **Note that this blessing prayer includes:**

- Joe's original design (*"… man of grace, compassion, and strength…"*)
- Impartation (*"I bless you with God's strength…I bless you with an increased ability to extend that grace and love to others."*)
- Specific replacement truths (*"…walk in forgiveness toward the people who have hurt you…"*)
- God's truth and character (*"You have God's unconditional love deeply rooted in your heart."*)

It may be appropriate, if the wound/love deficit/injustice is related to the person's relationship with his or her father, to ask a man of appropriate age to join the prayer team at the blessing stage (if there is not one already on the team) in order to pray a "father's blessing" over the person. Equally, if the prayer time has dealt with issues with the candidate's mother, it may be appropriate for a woman to speak a blessing.

IMPARTATION

To be pure and uncluttered vessels of God's love and power, we must make sure we are in touch with God, walking with Him, and hearing from the Holy Spirit to minister to one another. In the ministry of impartation we cannot give what we do not have (i.e., spiritual grace, anointing, power, etc.). Therefore, for us to be significantly used by God in ministering to others, we must continue to grow in our own intimacy with God in holiness and love. In Scripture, the ministry of impartation is shown to bring healing, commissioning, blessing, and Holy Spirit infilling, as demonstrated in the table on the next page (emphasis added to Scriptures):

> *To be pure and uncluttered vessels of God's love and power, we must make sure we are in touch with God, walking with Him, and hearing from the Holy Spirit to minister to one another.*

Commissioning and anointing for leadership and ministry	**Numbers 27:22-23** *So Moses did as the Lord commanded and presented Joshua to Eleazar the priest and the whole community. Moses <u>laid his hands on him</u> and commissioned him to his responsibilities, just as the Lord had commanded through Moses.* **Acts 13:3** *So after more fasting and prayer, <u>the men laid their hands on them and sent them on their way</u>.*
Imparting the Holy Spirit's filling	**Acts 8:17** *Then Peter and John <u>laid their hands upon these believers, and they received the Holy Spirit</u>.* **Acts 19:5-6** *As soon as they heard this, they were baptized in the name of the Lord Jesus. Then when Paul <u>laid his hands on them</u>, the Holy Spirit came on them, and they spoke in other tongues and prophesied.*
Healing	**Luke 4:40** *As the sun went down that evening, people throughout the village brought sick family members to Jesus. No matter what their diseases were, <u>the touch of His hand healed every one</u>.* **Acts 28:8** *As it happened, Publius's father was ill with fever and dysentery. Paul went in and prayed for him, <u>and laying his hands on him, he healed him</u>.*
Imparting spiritual gifts	**1 Timothy 4:14** *Do not neglect <u>the spiritual gift you received</u> through the prophecies spoken to you <u>when the elders of the church laid their hands on you</u>.*

IMPARTATIONAL PRAYER SHOULD INCLUDE:

1. prophetically affirming spiritual covering, blessings, identity, and destiny in prayer
2. encouraging, strengthening, and restoring the value of the person in God's eyes and affirming his or her role in His kingdom
3. replacing with truth the lies that have been believed
4. praying the prayer candidate's original design and biblical destiny over him or her, in terms of who he (or she) truly is and how God wants to bless and use him/her from now on
5. praying for him or her to be filled with God's Spirit in a fresh and increased measure
6. asking the Spirit to sharpen his or her conscience to be more sensitive to these strongholds playing out in the future
7. asking for empowering from the Holy Spirit to enable him or her to actively walk in the opposite spirit

8. praying God's deep healing to the person, filling the places where he or she has been wounded

These prayers can be like pouring gold into the empty places that have been left by the strongholds and lies. They are like filling a vacuum or releasing water over a desert. These words and prayers have huge significance to bring life to deep parts of people's souls. In them, we want to encourage people to live out of the deep place of meeting with God and living dependent on His Spirit and love, rather than striving to live differently out of their own strength.

LEAD THE PERSON IN PRAYERS OF DECLARATION, FAITH, AND THANKSGIVING

The prayer captain should:

1. Summarize the ministry that has just taken place in the person's life.
2. Encourage him or her to thank God for the work He did and will be faithful to perform. Have him or her declare in an affirmative way how God sees him or her at this time.
3. Have the prayer candidate affirm his or her commitment to walk in the truth that obliterates the strongholds exposed in the ministry session, in the power of the Holy Spirit, and in faithfulness to God. He or she should name specific areas of life and actions in which he or she will replace old patterns with new patterns of behavior through decisions of the will and the power of the Holy Spirit.

→ Help the prayer candidate pray in faith, not to pray "hope to" prayers.

→ Help him or her focus on what was done, not on what may remain.

→ Help him or her begin exercising his (or her) authority in Christ. Bind the enemy from bringing confusion.

FINAL WORDS OF PRACTICAL ENCOURAGEMENT AND EXHORTATION

1. Give the prayer candidate any follow-up material appropriate to the time. This might include stronghold inventories from the *Walking in Freedom* manual or referencing the stronghold sections in the back of the *Living Set Free Course Manual*.

2. Give him or her the notes from the prayer session, as directed by the captain. Always give the notes of original design/blessings/Scriptures. The captain may also sometimes elect to give the rest of the summarized notes of the session.

Strongly encourage the prayer candidate to participate in ministry and discipleship relationships and/or a church small group if possible, to find support and encouragement in his or her walk into freedom. Affirm the importance of submission to a local church spiritual authority as a primary spiritual covering.

PRACTICAL EXERCISE: Impartational Prayer

Each person in the group will receive prayer in response to the question asked of the Lord, *"Lord, how do you see this person today?"* The group should listen for words of comfort, strength, and encouragement (1 Cor. 14:3). Then, using the guidelines above, gather around the person receiving prayer, laying hands on him or her and praying a prayer of impartation and blessing related to what was received by the team.

Each person should receive 15 minutes of impartational prayer from the team.

1. As recommended in the last session, re-read this session after having prayed with your team and the prayer candidate for comfort, strength, and encouragement. Note any thoughts, impressions, or questions that come up in your mind as you do so.

2. In the *Walking in Freedom* manual or *Living Set Free Course Manual*, personally work through the stronghold sections assigned by your instructor.

{ SESSION SEVEN }
ROOTS AND FRUITS OF SPIRITUAL STRONGHOLDS

*Let your roots grow down into him, and let your lives be built on him.
Then your faith will grow strong in the truth you were taught,
and you will overflow with thankfulness.*
Colossians 2:7

The principle of "roots and fruits" works for both positive and negative strongholds in our lives. If we cultivate godly strongholds of right thinking and obedience, our lives will produce fruit in accordance with that—as the Scripture above points out. On the other hand, if we allow sin to go unchecked and ungodly strongholds develop, those, too, will produce fruit accordingly.

If we picture a stronghold like a tree, we can imagine that the patterns of behavior we see in people's lives are like the branches and fruit. The "core" (or main) stronghold(s) would be the trunk of the tree. The roots would be the source from which the stronghold has developed and which continues to "feed it." The diagram on the next page gives an analogous structure of strongholds in a person's life.

Simply trying to tackle the obvious, surface patterns of behavior in our lives (the "fruit"), repenting of those and trying hard to live differently, is like trimming branches and plucking fruit—which quickly just grow back. If we really want to get rid of them and be who God has created us to be, we need to identify and pull up the trunk and the roots of the tree, not just focus on the branches. We will find that once we have dealt with the roots and trunk, the branches and fruit will fall away more easily.

Notes:

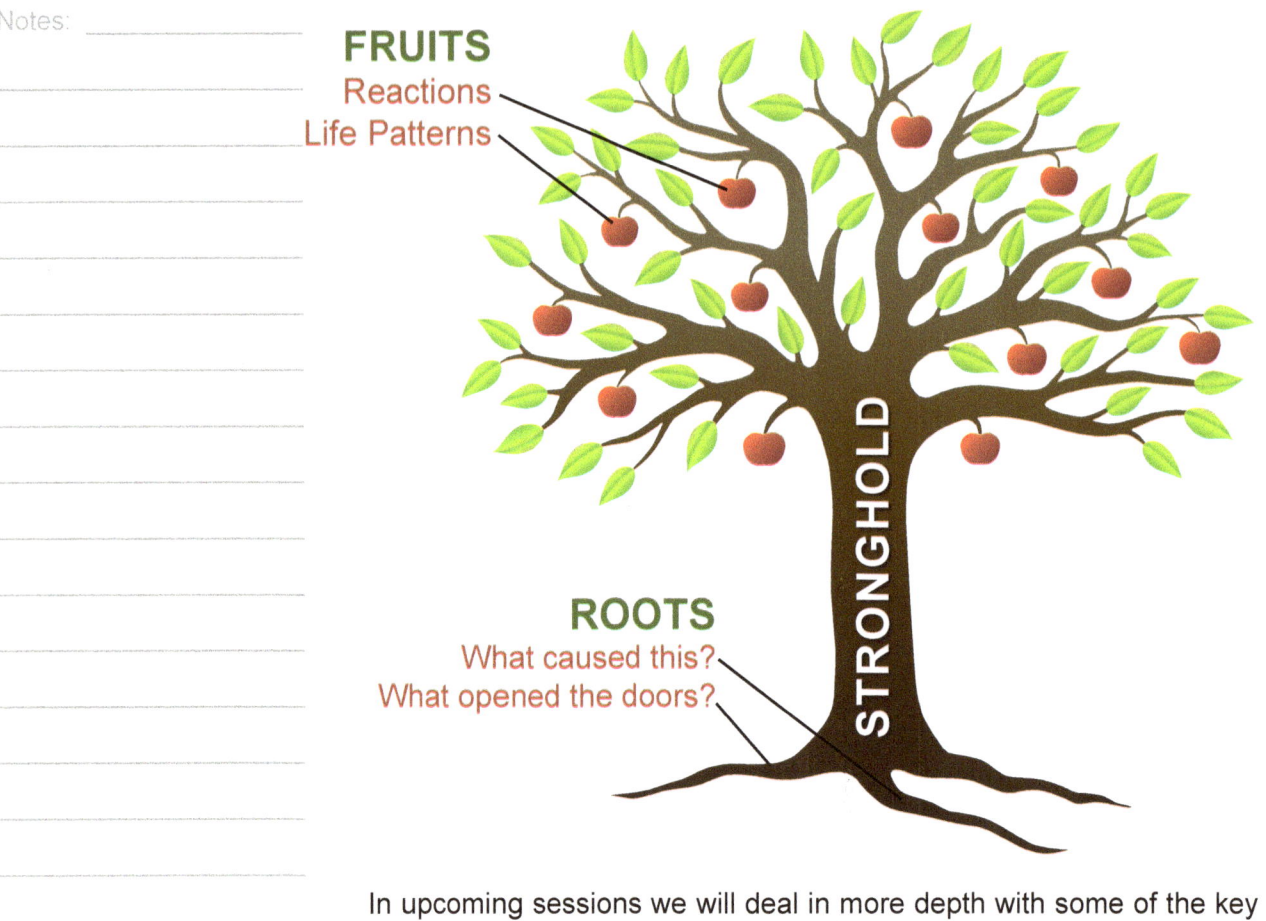

In upcoming sessions we will deal in more depth with some of the key "roots" of strongholds such as injustices, love deficits, generational strongholds, soul-ties, curses and occult activity. Pulling up these roots usually requires helping prayer candidates to grant forgiveness as well as take responsibility for (and repent of) their own sin reactions.

IDENTIFYING STRONGHOLDS

Revelation of the Core Stronghold(s)

This step of the ministry time typically begins with the captain inquiring of the Lord in order to gain revelation about the core stronghold(s) and the way these are played out in the person's life. This is to identify the trunk, branches, and fruit, of the tree in our illustration. Some example questions are given below:

QUESTION #1

"Lord, what are the core stronghold issues you want to address in this prayer time?"

Scenario: For the sake of demonstration, let's say the team receives *anger, rejection,* and *bitterness.*

These would be words, pictures, mental images, examples of Bible characters, etc. about behavior patterns or attitudes that would help the person to recognize the strongholds in his or her life.

QUESTION #2

If the team receives multiple strongholds the captain then might ask,
"Lord, is there an order you want us to pursue in addressing these strongholds, or what is the core stronghold?"

It is helpful to discern which one(s) is the core or primary stronghold(s) and which are secondary. This can be done by experience and discernment. Using the example from the above question #1, we know that "anger" is a secondary emotion or reaction. Therefore the other stronghold received ('rejection") is most likely the primary or core stronghold. A second and a most effective way to ascertain the core stronghold is through prayer. Ask the Lord to reveal to you which of the strongholds received is the core stronghold. Below is a sample question.

QUESTION #3

At the same time as the first question, the captain may also ask:
"How do these strongholds play out or manifest in this person's life?"

Once the revelation has been received and the listeners have submitted on paper their revelation to the captain, the captain will discern what to share with the person receiving prayer and how to share it. It is best if the person does not recognize the stronghold(s) shared, that the captain can ask the person's permission to ask the Lord for further clarification and revelation regarding what it looks like. This can be done by asking the Lord to more specifically reveal patterns of behavior or expressions of the strongholds in the person's life.

Remember it is important that we move forward in each step of the ministry time with the person only as he or she has revelation in what has been received by the prayer team and with his or her permission.

Revelation of the Roots

During this part of the prayer time, someone may receive revelation that there is a certain type of root or access point at play. The most common roots of spiritual strongholds are love/truth deficits, injustices, generational issues, curses, soul-ties, and the person's own outright sin.

The following is an example of a question to ask the Lord in seeking to understand any root or source to a stronghold that is at play in a person's life.

QUESTION #4 (THE "ROOT")

"Lord, what is the primary access point(s) or root(s) the enemy energizes in regards to the stronghold of _____?"

Note: some of these potential issues will be covered in-depth in later sessions. For now they serve as examples of the kinds of access points that may be at the root of certain stronghold issues.

Injustices/Truth-deficit

If "injustice" is received, supplementary questions might be:

- *What was the injustice in this person's life that is at the root of the stronghold(s) revealed?*
- *What are this person's sin reaction(s) to this injustice?*
- *Is there a lie believed about himself/herself, or about You, Lord?*

If there is a truth deficit, there will be a "core lie" the person believes and out of which the person lives life. After the revelation has been received and offered to the person, allow the person to process and briefly respond explaining how it is relevant to his or her life and experience.

Love-deficit / Truth-deficit

withholding
no blessings spoken
lack of affirmation

If "love-deficit" is received, supplementary questions might be:

- *What was the love deficit in this person's life that is at the root of the stronghold(s) revealed?*
- *What are this person's sin reaction(s) to this love-deficit?*
- *Is there a lie believed about himself/herself, or about You, Lord?*

A core lie is a heartfelt belief about the person or about God that is not in line with God's truth. An example is that he or she may have projected the imperfect character of a parent or another authority figure onto God, for example "God's love for me is conditional; I need to earn it."

When sharing this revelation it is important again to use questions. For example, "How would you describe your relationship with your parents when you were growing up?" or "How would you characterize your parents speaking words of life and affirming you when you as a child?"

Outright Sin

The access point for a stronghold might be outright sin that the person has been living in that is not related to a specific injustice. This could include any kind of sin – including lying, sexual sin, or involvement with the occult, etc.

Generational Issues

If "generational issues" are received, supplementary questions might be:

- *From which side of the family was this stronghold passed down? (maybe both)*
- *What was the entry point or conception of this stronghold into the family?*

It may not be possible for the person receiving ministry to know for certain the source of the generational issue(s) received. But they might readily recognize the symptomatic by-product(s) in his or her family. After the revelation has been offered, allow the person to briefly respond explaining what patterns he or she sees in his or her family. From the obvious evidences they can address those generational issues in faith.

Curses

If "curses" is received, supplementary questions might be:

- *What curses are active?*
- *What is/are the source(s) of the curse(s) or how was the curse conceived?*

The person receiving ministry might not be able to know for certain the source of a curse(s). You would then proceed similar to the above "generational issue".

Soul-ties

If "soul-tie" is received, supplementary questions might be:

- *Who is the soul-tie with?*
- *What is the source of this soul-tie?*
- *What have been the evidences of this person's soul tie(s)?*

If the soul-tie is with a person in which the Scriptures speak of a legitimate soul-bond (i.e. spouse, parents, children, etc.), it is important to emphasize that in severing the soul-ties we are not cutting off our relationship with them. Rather they will be cutting off inappropriate dependence or negative influence(s) through the spiritually energized soul-tie(s). All that is biblically appropriate in the relationship remains.

PRACTICAL EXERCISE: Exposing Roots of a Core Stronghold

A true revelation of God's love for a person, and the power that comes from that love, is often impeded by love deficits and injustices in the person's lives and by their own sin reactions to these situations. True freedom comes to people as they repent of their sin reactions in prayer and extend forgiveness to their offenders.

Depending on the time available today one or two people in the group will receive prayer concerning the roots and fruits of a core stronghold standing against walking in God's original design (there should have been a core stronghold identified in an earlier prayer time).

We will set aside two 30-minute sessions to pray for two people, 30 minutes for each person. We will simply ask the Lord what love deficit(s) or injustice(s) He wants to deal with today and what sin reactions have developed in this person's life as a result.

You may also elect to pray with just one person for one hour, in order to be more thorough; however, if you do so, recognize that everyone will not receive prayer during this session and will need to receive ministry sometime this week.

You again will work with an experienced prayer team minister(s) in your group of four.

Conducting the Session

You always need to approach your training prayer sessions as REAL prayer times, not just "practice" sessions. The spiritual transactions your prayer candidates are making are just as significant and important as any other, regardless of the fact that you are in training.

Before you begin your prayer session, remember to:

- Prepare the ministry team spiritually.
- Seal off the room and the session in prayer, taking authority over any perceived or potential activity of the enemy and inviting the presence of the Holy Spirit.

- Greet and prepare your prayer candidate.

(refer to Session One of Prayer Team Training "A," if review is needed on the above procedure)

The captain will inquire of the Lord using the following questions:

"How does the identified stronghold play out practically in this person's life?"(fruits)

"Is there an injustice or love/truth deficit at the root(s) of this stronghold?"

Lead the person through a prayer transaction related to the roots, stronghold(s) and sin reactions.

Then close with a prayer of impartation over him or her, including specific truths, pictures, words, etc. received.

NOTE: **In this session be alert to the time that is allotted.** The total time of this exercise for each person should not take more than 30 minutes if two persons are receiving prayer in this exercise hour, and not more than 60 minutes if one person is receiving prayer. There might be the need for a follow-up prayer session if everything revealed was not able to be finished up due to time limitations.

THE 4 Rs

1) **REPENT**
(of the sin or the lie)

2) **REBUKE**
(the work and influence of the enemy)

3) **REPLACE**
(the behavior or lie) with obedience and truth

4) **RECEIVE**
(God's forgiveness and the Holy Spirit's infilling)

1. As recommended in the last session, re-read this session after having prayed with your team and a prayer candidate regarding one core stronghold. Note any thoughts, impressions, or questions that come up in your mind as you do so.

2. Prepare for the next session of your training by reading "Session Eight: Strongholds of Injustice and Love Deficit."

3. In the *Walking in Freedom* manual, personally work through the following sections of Injustice and Love Deficit. As you read, remember to be asking the Lord, *"What are You showing me about me?"*

{ SESSION EIGHT }
STRONGHOLDS OF INJUSTICE AND LOVE DEFICIT

May you have the power to understand, as all God's people should, how wide, how long, how high and how deep his love is. May you experience the love of Christ, though it is too great to understand fully. Then you will be made complete with all the fullness of life and power that comes from God.
Ephesians 3:18-20

Love deficits and injustices will often surface when we are discerning from God the "root" or access point of a person's strongholds. When someone has not received God's quality of love, especially from authority figures such as parents, he is living in "love deficit" or "love deprivation." Even if parents do love a child and have not intended any harm, ways in which their love and actions have not mirrored God's love can result in a perceived loss of significance, security, value and self worth. This is even more the case if there has been abandonment, an active withdrawing of love, or acts of cruelty and/or abuse.

The enemy uses these wounds to reinforce the idea that people are fundamentally unloved, unlovable, and unimportant. If Satan succeeds in disrupting and damaging the quality of love people receive from others, especially authority figures and parents, this can easily be twisted and projected so that their perception of God's love for them is also damaged and distorted.

Many people do not recognize that they are living in a state of love deprivation. Most people, when an area of love deprivation is revealed in a prayer time, think that the level and quality of love and affection they experienced is fairly typical. Yet, in reality, there have been

marked levels of love deprivation; they have just learned to cope and compensate for the resulting emotional damage. Over these wounds, the enemy builds self-comforting strongholds rooted in sin responses to the injustices and love/truth deficits that people have experienced. Many times the fruits of these strongholds will appear as besetting sins and negative personality characteristics with which they battle, unsuccessfully, for much or even all of their lives. But when these roots are exposed to the Truth and Light of God's love, people can be powerfully set free!

THE LOVE GOD INTENDS FOR US

God intends for people to receive His lavish love fully, and to receive "100% God-quality love" from those around them, starting with parents and siblings. To see where their human relationships may have fallen short, your prayer candidates first need to understand the nature of God's love for them.

As a freedom prayer team minister, it is crucial for you to be very familiar with the principles and Scriptures that affirm God's great love for His children, as it is one of the truths most viciously opposed by the enemy in people's lives. For a more thorough treatment of the truths about God's quality of love (and what it ought to look like in human relationships), please review the last half of Session 4 in the *Living Set Free Course Manual*.

LOVE DEFICIT

It is important in this portion of a freedom prayer session (i.e. exposing the roots of injustice and love deficit) that we do not encourage prayer candidates to unearth childhood memories and wounds so as to live self-focused and introspective lives, or to deflect personal responsibility onto others for how they live. We simply want to determine where the enemy has gained territory in their lives to keep them from fully receiving God's love, and help them walk back into the love and power that comes from that truth. To do this, we need to understand where the enemy has gained access to these territories in the first place, in order to remove the roots and dismantle the resulting strongholds.

TYPES OF LOVE DEPRIVATION

While not exhaustive, below are brief descriptions of various expressions of love deprivation. These will help in discerning and explaining to others what love deprivation might look like in their lives.

1. Rejection

Rejection is characterized by various forms of dismissal, denial, and denunciation. It is a refusal to accept a person with full appreciation. Anything less than 100 percent delight, affirmation, and healthy connectedness results in various measures of feeling rejected.

2. Abandonment

To abandon is to forsake someone or something, to withdraw one's attention, protection, support, and/or interest. When parents are absent (maybe even not necessarily through their own fault), that is a form of abandonment. Sometimes one parent or another might leave a family or cease to actively engage in and perform the responsibilities that a parent should toward a child. The same thing can happen toward a spouse. Good friends can abandon friends. Church leaders may abandon churches and churches their church leaders. If a child experienced a period of being separated from parents due to illness, military service, or boarding school they may feel a sense of abandonment. The death of a parent or grandparent (or other significant figure in a person's life) can also lead to a sense of abandonment.

3. Withholding

To withhold is to hold back, to refrain from giving. Withholding does not seem like a tragic sin, but it is actually quite devastating. It creates a vacuum that many times is filled with crippling doubts and lies from the enemy. When parents, spouses, and leaders neglect a person/child or hold back love, attention, affirmation, affection, and words of blessing —when they fail to speak truth and God's destiny into people's lives—these people are damaged by love deprivation.

4. Abuse

Many people experience abuse in their lives— abuse being to injure or damage, treat cruelly or roughly, or mistreat. This can include physical, verbal, sexual, spiritual, mental, and emotional abuse (including authoritarianism) —all of which affect the very core of a person's being. This can often leave a person with a sense of shame and worthlessness, and a belief that he or she is unlovable or was to blame in some way for the abuse.

5. Control

Some people live with a powerful need to regulate and control the people and/or circumstances around them in seemingly every matter. This

Notes:

© 2024 SycPub Global, LLC. All Rights Reserved. Do not reprint without prior written permission.

might range from situations that can seem innocuous (such as parents who have an inordinate need to make decisions for their children) to obviously dangerous situations such as cult leaders (who control the lives and often the thinking of their members). This could take many forms such as a dominating parent or teacher who elicits fear of punishment, or a smothering parent who is overly emotional, needy, or demanding. Those who live in excessively controlling environments live under a constant pressure that can make them feel threatened, insecure, suppressed, and manipulated.

6. Shame

Shame is a defeating and painful emotion. Sometimes people have been controlled or disciplined by shame—literally bullied by guilt and condemnation into compliance characterized by disgrace and humiliation. This brings about deep feelings of guilt and unworthiness which in turn lead to self-hatred.

7. Conditional/performance based love

When love and acceptance are held back until the behavior or performance is acceptable based on certain expectations, the response can include a sense of inadequacy, unworthiness, striving, comparison, and rebellion.

EXPOSING LOVE DEFICITS IN A PRAYER SESSION

People will often find it hard to recognize a love deficit, especially when it relates to a parent. Most people accept their parental situation as normal and may even put their parents on a pedestal, beyond criticism. They may feel that identifying a love deficit in some way betrays and dishonors their parents and denies all the good things they good do and give. Especially if people have Christian or "good" parents, they may find it hard to see there was anything lacking.

In this component of freedom prayer ministry, we are not endeavoring to bring up love deficits that were not there to begin with. However, if there has been a deficit it does need to be recognized in order for the person to be freed to receive God's love more fully.

At this point in the session, after collecting the revelation from the listeners, if the captain sees there is evidence of love deprivation, he or she can gently help the person to gain revelation themselves by asking questions such as, "How would you describe your relationship with _____?" or "With what words and in what ways did _____ bless you when you were growing up?"

If the prayer candidate is still not able to recognize any love deficit, do not push it; the Holy Spirit may bring him to a point of revelation later and he can pray about it at that time.

INJUSTICES

The gateway to freedom from the impact of injustices in our lives is the divinely powerful weapon of forgiveness.

A crucial aspect of ministering freedom and restoration is helping people release the anger, bitterness, resentment, and sometimes even soul-ties associated with injustices and abuses they have encountered in the course of their lives.

TYPES OF INJUSTICE

Injustices, tragically, can take many forms. You will find an inventory of injustices in the Appendix of this manual, but for now, here is a brief list:

- Trauma/accidents/injuries/ illness/ death of a loved one
- Affairs/divorce/separation
- Abandonment by a parent
- High expectations
- Favoritism towards siblings
- Verbal/emotional/physical/sexual/spiritual abuse
- Drug/alcohol/pornography use in home
- Harsh, violent or manipulative discipline
- Response to illness or handicap
- Insecure/unstable home life – moving home/school/ city/ church
- Discrimination or bullying
- Withholding/ being overlooked/conditional love
- Not receiving recognition/reward that was due

EXPOSING INJUSTICES IN A FREEDOM PRAYER SESSION

The gateway to freedom from the impact of injustices in our lives is the divinely powerful weapon of forgiveness. People need to recognize their own sinful responses to the injustices (or love deficits, as the case may be). They need to own them as their own sin, repent of them, take back the territory the enemy has built on them, and replace the lies and sinful reactions with God's truth.

In a prayer time, when asking God about roots of strongholds (including injustices and love deficits) the captain should ask the listeners to write down what they receive and give it to the captain.

© 2024 SycPub Global, LLC. All Rights Reserved. Do not reprint without prior written permission.

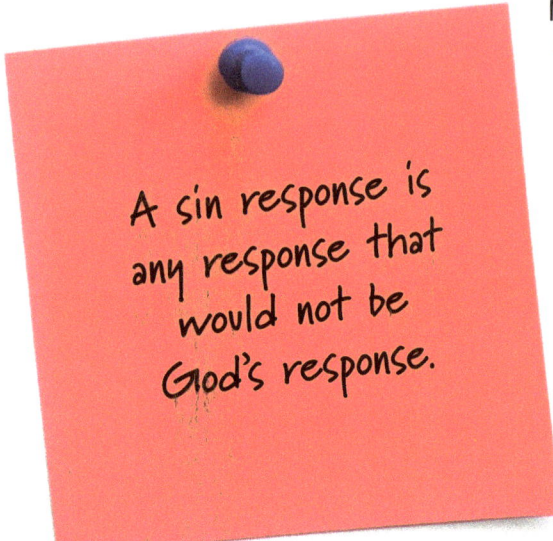

A sin response is any response that would not be God's response.

Many times the Holy Spirit will speak in mental pictures and images that may be overwhelming or confusing to the prayer candidate if the listeners were to share them directly. The captain can read the listeners' notes in order to discern what he or she will (and will not) share with the person receiving prayer.

The revelation may seem vague or piecemeal (e.g. a picture of a child afraid in a small room, or words like "mother" or "negative words from an authority figure"). The captain can share these insights humbly and simply, without attempt at interpretation by the prayer team. The words and pictures may trigger the prayer candidate to fill in the gaps of what issues require forgiveness and prayer.

IDENTIFYING AND DEALING WITH SIN RESPONSES TO LOVE DEFICITS AND INJUSTICES

If people do not receive significance, security, and worth legitimately as God designed them to, from Him and from loving human relationships, then they will often seek it illegitimately in ways that are sinful. This can be either to comfort themselves and dampen their sense of rejection, insignificance or abandonment, or to illicitly capture love, value, and worth. It can also include coping mechanisms and self-protective measures such as control or withholding. **A sin response is any response that would not be God's response.**

These responses can become so deeply ingrained that they become ways of life, and some people even mistakenly believe that they are part of their character. This is why people often find it hard to recognize these sin responses themselves. A freedom prayer time can lovingly bring these into the light in order to break their power.

EXAMPLES OF SIN REACTIONS

- Fear
- Control
- Striving
- Anger
- Bitterness
- Self-pity
- Ungodly sorrow
- Inappropriate guilt/shame
- Insignificance/worthlessness
- Self-hatred
- Distrust of authority
- Passivity
- Drugs/alcohol/eating disorders
- Sexual promiscuity

**INJUSTICE RECEIVED:
HURT & OFFENDED**

REPEATED WOUNDS & DAMAGE

UNGODLY REACTION, UNHEALTHY PATTERNS DEVELOP

OTHERS REACT WITH SINFUL RESPONSES

BEHAVIOR CAUSES OFFENSE TO OTHERS

When people are living in unhealthy and ungodly patterns of behavior in reaction to injustices, this can result in repeated wounds and damage due to others' reactions to their sinful responses. This can become a destructive cycle.

EXPOSING SIN RESPONSES IN A PRAYER SESSION

Even though in some ways these sinful responses to injustices or love deficits may seem understandable or even "natural," they go against God's truth for life. People need to identify them and "own" them, taking responsibility for their sin in repentance. None of us can blame our circumstances or other people for our own sin responses. Each of us has a choice regarding how we respond to injustices. Jesus certainly experienced injustice and yet He never sinned.

1 Peter 2:23 NIV
When they hurled their insults at him, he did not retaliate; when he suffered, he made no threats. Instead, he entrusted himself to him who judges justly.

When the prayer team receives revelation concerning particular sin responses to injustices, the captain can gently probe for more clarity through the use of strategic questions. Some examples might be:

"Did you feel any pressure to be perfect?"

Was anger expressed in your family and/or toward you? If so how?

In this process, help the person guard against self-condemnation. Emphasize that the purpose of recognizing the sin is not to dwell on it, but rather to deal with it and move into the freedom God has for him or her. Point out that God is not shocked by the candidate's sinful response to the injustice(s). He is mindful of our frame; He knows that we are "but dust" (Ps. 103:14). Stress the fact that God wants to set him or her free from the enemy's ways of responding to injustices (which only cause more pain), and release him or her to experience complete peace, joy, forgiveness, and freedom.

People may become defensive at this point, arguing that it is "natural" to react to circumstances in the way they have. However, if the response is not how God would have reacted, and if it is outside God's truth and intention for our lives, then it is sin. For example, it is right to grieve the loss of a loved one. However, if the grief extends over an inappropriate length of time and makes a person bitter, self-absorbed, and unable to see and receive God's blessing and comfort, then it has become unhealthy/ungodly sorrow.

PATTERNS & EXPRESSIONS OF SIN RESPONSES

If the person finds it hard to recognize the sin response that has been received by the prayer team, ask permission to go back to prayer and ask the Holy Spirit for patterns and expressions of a stronghold so the person might recognize it. **If he or she still doesn't recognize or receive it, move on and only pray through the sin responses he or she recognizes and agrees with. He (or she) may recognize the others later and can pray through them at that time.**

TRUTH DEFICITS

WORLDVIEW

Satan is the father of lies (Jn. 8:44) and constantly seeks to sow lies into people's lives: lies about themselves and about God. Lies have huge power over us since we all live life according to our perception of reality.

Satan's lies can be cognitive (in one's head) rooted in humanistic teaching and cultural, family, or religious worldviews. They can also be emotional—lies of the heart which are rooted in our emotions and hidden memories of the past. Either way, under the influence of these lies, people often grow up believing untruths about life, the world, people or God. These lies may have been spoken audibly and drummed into them repeatedly by a parent or authority figure. They may have simply been implied by actions or inaction. However they were received, the person begins to believe the untruths to be truth, which will affect the way they live their lives. Some examples of truth deficits are:

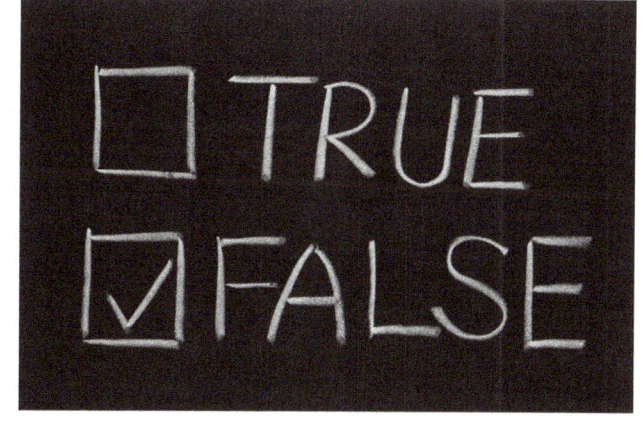

- "You can't trust anyone."
- "You never get anything without deserving it."
- "You must be in a relationship to be worth something."
- "Anyone who believes in God is a fool."
- "God is strict. You must do penance to appease Him."

It is important to recognize particular lies where the person may have projected the fallible love they have received from authority figures onto God. This is particularly the case regarding relationships with fathers. For example, if a person's father was emotionally distant, he or she may subconsciously believe that God is distant and uninterested, and relate to Him accordingly.

WORD CURSES

A word curse is a negative statement spoken to or over a person, which sows a lie into his heart, and curses him to live according to the resulting "lie" believed about himself (or herself). The person speaking the words often does not realize the evil impact of the words on that person's life. We are not speaking here of curses of witchcraft, but often the careless words of a parent, relative, teacher, spouse, or friend. For example:

- "You'll never amount to anything."
- "You are a burden."
- "You aren't worth much."
- "You must achieve to be valuable."
- "You are not lovable."

As a result of these kinds of word curses, core lies can be developed in the heart of a person. The person is often not consciously aware that he or she believes that lie, but his (or her) actions and life are affected by it. Often there are two key related lies: a lie about themselves and a lie about God. For example:

- "I am not important enough to be blessed" or "I am unlovable."
- "God is always interested in other people, not me" or "God is not trustworthy."

© 2024 SycPub Global, LLC. All Rights Reserved. Do not reprint without prior written permission.

We appropriate God's freedom from the enemy's lies through truth. It is truth that destroys the hold the enemy has over us.

John 8:32 (NIV)
Then you will know the truth and the truth will set you free.

ADDRESSING INJUSTICES AND LOVE/TRUTH DEFICITS

In a freedom prayer ministry session, in order to address injustices/love deficits and our prayer candidates' sinful responses to them, we as prayer teams need to help them:

- **Acknowledge** the real and painful sin against them
- **Grant forgiveness** and bless those that hurt them
- **Repent** of their sin responses
- **Rebuke** in Christ's authority any evil spirit or scheme of the enemy related to the sin responses and break any lies they have believed.
- **Replace** the sin responses and lies with God's truth.
- **Receive** God's healing and comfort by His Holy Spirit and claim in faith that whatever Satan meant for harm, God is now going to use for fruitfulness.

FORGIVENESS

Helping people pray through and extend forgiveness toward those who have hurt them is a key component of freedom prayer ministry, particularly when it comes to dealing with love deficits and injustices. There are many misconceptions regarding forgiveness that can hold people back from forgiving and from the resulting freedom they can gain. It is essential that we as prayer teams understand what forgiveness is (and what it is not), and are able to explain this clearly and succinctly to people during a prayer time, especially if someone is struggling to forgive.

1. WHY FORGIVENESS IS IMPORTANT

If we do not forgive, we are trapped, chained to the person who has done us wrong. This lack of freedom affects us more than it affects the perpetrator of the injustice. People often ask, "Why should I forgive/release them? They don't deserve it." Actually, it is more us than the other person whom we are releasing. If we do not forgive, we limit the flow of power and love of God's Holy Spirit into our lives.

Forgiveness is not an option for Christians; it's a commandment—and is essential to people pulling up significant roots of sinful attitudes in their lives. For example, if a father has been emotionally withdrawn and not given words of affection, and his child has reacted with sin responses related to insignificance, this love deficit needs to be forgiven by the child before he or she can powerfully attack and root out the insignificance.

Colossians 3:13 (NIV)
Bear with each other and forgive whatever grievances you may have against one another. Forgive as the Lord forgave you.

2. WHAT FORGIVENESS IS AND IS NOT

People often say, "But you don't understand how much this person hurt me." God's commandment to forgive does not mean denying the hurt or saying it was okay. Forgiveness is releasing oneself from the impact of and sinful responses to that hurt.

FORGIVENESS IS NOT:
- approving of, excusing or justifying what the person did
- rationalizing or explaining the person's behavior
- saying the offense was okay or isn't important
- pretending we were not hurt or angry

FORGIVENESS IS:
- giving up our "right" to:
  - judge or punish the offender(s)
  - make them pay
  - make them realize they were wrong
  - bitterness
  - feelings of responsibility to make them change or repent
- entrusting offenders into God's hands, to God's judgment, not ours
- choosing to stop withholding blessing, affirmation, and love from offenders

3. GRANTING FORGIVENESS IN A PRAYER SESSION

The captain may offer to lead the person through the forgiveness prayer, establishing first the name of the person he or she is forgiving, or the term he uses for that person if it is a family member (e.g. "Dad," "Grandpa," "Nana," Uncle Joe," etc.).

It can be helpful for the prayer candidate to imagine and address the person he or she needs to forgive as if that person were in the room. This can help the prayer candidate engage in his heart and not just his head, so that it is not just words or a religious formula. However, this is not essential. If the person is not comfortable with this, he can simply address God in prayer, telling God he forgives the other person.

> *True freedom comes when people repent of sin responses in prayer and extend forgiveness to their offenders.*

After the prayer candidate has articulated his (or her) granting of forgiveness, it is important to replace the vacuum left by the departing bitterness with blessing instead. This means the forgiver chooses and determines to:

- bless the offender, in prayer and in his/her mind and words
- treat the offender with respect and kindness
- not rehearse the offense in his/her thoughts or conversations with others
- not necessarily have to tell the offender he/she has forgiven (unless he or she feels God has particularly asked him or her to do so)
- have a change in attitude and behavior towards the offender

Additional names of people the prayer candidate needs to forgive may emerge during the process of recognizing and praying through his or her love deficits and injustices. If this happens, the captain should point these out and have the prayer candidate pray through forgiving these people during the replacement portion of the 4R prayer.

It is possible to pray a prayer of forgiveness regarding someone who has died. In that instance, the prayer captain should encourage the person to address God in the prayer rather than addressing the person directly. For the blessing portion of such a transaction, it is appropriate for the prayer candidate to bless that person's memory, and the fruit of his or her life.

It is important to ensure that the person actually *says* "I forgive you" or "I forgive my dad," rather than "I want to forgive you" or "Lord, help me to forgive him." Desiring to forgive or praying about it is not the same as actually *doing* it.

After forgiving someone, it is often necessary for the prayer candidate to break a soul-tie with that person. This will be examined in Session Eight.

It should be explained to the prayer candidate that after he or she has forgiven, although a real and significant spiritual transaction has taken place, feelings of bitterness and anger may well up again. If this happens, he or she should not be discouraged. He (or she) may need to continue to forgive. It can be a step-by-step process as people acknowledge each level of pain. Jesus commanded his disciples to forgive as many times as seventy times seven (Mt. 18:22).

4. EXAMPLE OF A FORGIVENESS PRAYER

a. Recognize the hurt of the offense

"Lord, I recognize and bring into the light, the sin done against me by _____ (Address the person, imagine them in front of you). _____,

I recognize you have sinned against me, you have.... (encourage the person to describe the offense committed against him and explain in his own words how it made him feel. "What you did was wrong and it hurt me deeply.")

b. Cancel the debt/forgive

"Because of what Jesus has done for me, today I choose to cancel the debt you owe me. _____ , I forgive you. I release you from my judgment and place you into God's hands. I choose to move on in my life in obedience to God. In the name of Jesus, I sever the destructive soul-tie with you and any inappropriate influence you have over me."

c. Bless

"I bless you in the name of Jesus (encourage the prayer candidate to use his or her own words to bless the person he/she is forgiving).

True revelation of God's love for a person, and the power that comes from that love, is often impeded by love deficits and injustices in people's lives and by their own sin responses to these situations. True freedom comes when people repent of these sin responses in prayer and extend forgiveness to their offenders.

PRACTICAL EXERCISE: Exposing and Healing Roots of Injustice and Love Deficit

Depending on the time available, today two people in the group will receive prayer for an injustice or love deficit they have experienced in their lives. We will set aside two 30-minute sessions to pray for two people, 30 minutes for each person. We will simply ask the Lord what love deficit or injustice He wants to deal with today and what sin reactions have developed in this person's life as a result.

You may also elect to pray with just one person for one hour, in order to be more thorough; however if you do so, recognize that everyone will not receive prayer this week. Be sure to choose first any trainees who did not receive prayer the previous week.

CONDUCTING THE SESSION

Always approach your training prayer sessions as REAL prayer times, not just "practice" sessions. The spiritual transactions your prayer candidates are making are just as significant and important as any other, regardless of the fact that you are all in training.

1. Before you begin your prayer session, remember to:

    ☑ Prepare the ministry team spiritually.
    ☑ Seal off the room and the session in prayer, taking authority over any perceived or potential activity of the enemy and inviting the presence of the Holy Spirit.
    ☑ Greet and prepare your prayer candidate.

(refer to Session Seven, if review is needed on the above procedure)

NOTE: **In this session be alert to the time that is allotted.** The total time of this exercise for each person should not take more than 30 minutes.

THIS SESSION'S PRACTICAL EXERCISE

1. The captain should inquire of the Lord on behalf of the team, asking the following questions:

"What love deficit or injustice in this person's life do you want to address today?" (In this session, please limit responses to one key injustice or love deficit. If listeners receive more than that, the captain should discern and decide which one to share).

"What are xx(the person's name)'s sin responses out of that situation?" (Here identify one or two core sin responses/strongholds and how they play out practically.)

2. Lead the person through the prayer transaction as described in the session: forgiveness and then the 4R's.

While the captain is leading the person through this prayer, the listeners can ask and listen to the Holy Spirit for insights and Scriptures related to specific truths for replacing the sin reactions and lies the candidate identified and renounced during the prayer time.

3. Pray a prayer of impartation over the person receiving prayer, including specific truths received.

1. As recommended last session, re-read this session after having prayed with your team and a prayer candidate regarding one key injustice or love deficit. Note any thoughts, impressions, or questions that come up in your mind as you do so.

2. Prepare for the next session of your training by reading Session Nine: Understanding and Attacking Generational Attachments.

{ SESSION NINE }
UNDERSTANDING AND ATTACKING GENERATIONAL ATTACHMENTS

You must not bow down to them or worship them, for I, the Lord your God, am a jealous God who will not tolerate your affection for any other gods. I lay the sins of the parents upon their children; the entire family is affected—even children in the third and fourth generations of those who reject me. 10 But I lavish unfailing love for a thousand generations on those[a] who love me and obey my commands.
Deuteronomy 5:9-10 NLT

Many times as the prayer team seeks the Lord for the roots of various stronghold issues in people's lives, it will emerge that the root is a *generational* stronghold.

Generational sin patterns and strongholds are family issues, learned and/or spiritually inherited, that can be traced through a family lineage. These might be patterns of attitude and thought, besetting sins, recurring illnesses, or behaviors that seem to recur from generation to generation. A generational stronghold may cause a person to be predisposed to certain behaviors or emotions that have little or no logical explanation in the natural realm, because they come from strongholds which were established in previous generations.

Recognizing the reality and seriousness of generational shadows is not fatalism, nor is it pointing the finger at family members or church/community leaders for past sins. It does not excuse us from responsibility for our own sin. Rather it is a place to begin, in humility and faith, the process of repentance and prayer so that we, our families, our churches, and our communities can start to set a new pattern of blessing for future generations.

Because we believe we have authority in Christ over these generational strongholds, just as we do over other strongholds in our lives, this can be a truly powerful and exciting turning point. Some of the most dramatic breakthroughs experienced in freedom prayer ministry have been through breaking generational strongholds and curses.

THE REALITY OF GENERATIONAL STRONGHOLDS

THE BIBLICAL WORLDVIEW ON GENERATIONAL RELATIONSHIPS

The Scriptures clearly state that the consequences of sin can be suffered by up to three or four subsequent generations.

Exodus 20:5 6 (NIV)
You shall not bow down to them or worship them; for I, the LORD your God, am a jealous God, <u>punishing the children for the sin of the fathers to the third and fourth generation</u> of those who hate me, but showing love to a thousand generations of those who love me and keep my commandments (emphasis added).

In God's grace, the blessings are stronger and pass down a thousand generations (Ex. 20:6; Deut. 5:10). However, the general principle is the same: our actions not only affect us and our own relationship with God, but will impact those who follow on after us. Of course, the Bible emphasizes that each individual is responsible before God for his or her own sin (Ez. 18:4, Rom. 6:23, 14:10) but we also can live in the "shadows" (strongholds) or the "light" (blessings) of the generations before us. Similarly, our future generations will either live in our shadows or our light.

BIBLICAL ACCOUNTS

Famine in David's Reign

There are many accounts in the Bible which demonstrate the reality of this principle. For example, the famine in David's reign was due to King Saul's sin (2 Sam. 21:1-14). A covenant had been made with the Gibeonites by Joshua that Israel would preserve the Gibeonites and not kill them (Josh. 21: 16-21). Years later, King Saul killed some of the Gibeonites, breaking the covenant made before God and therefore invoking God's judgment on Israel. The punishment continued after Saul's death, bringing a famine on the land.

Achan

In another account, Israel as a nation was suffering for the sin of Achan in Joshua 7. Achan took some plunder from Jericho, which God had forbidden Israel to do. The whole community of the nation of Israel was affected by the sin of Achan.

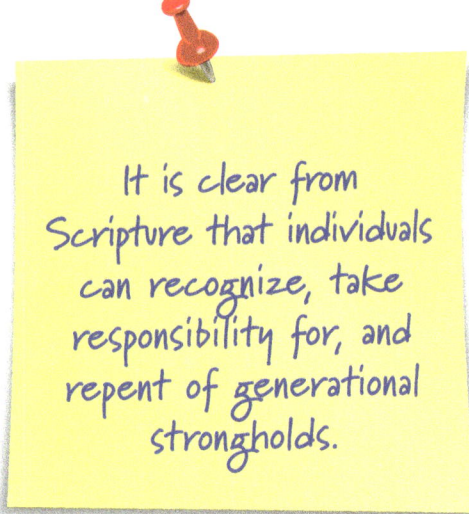

It is clear from Scripture that individuals can recognize, take responsibility for, and repent of generational strongholds.

Solomon's grandson, Abijam

Solomon's grandson Abijam was a further example of the sins of the father being repeated in the son's life.

1 Kings 15:3 (NIV)
[Abijam, Solomon's grandson] committed all the sins his father had done before him; his heart was not fully devoted to the LORD his God, as the heart of David his forefather had been (emphasis added).

Israel in exile

Israel recognized this generational reality. When they were in exile, they recognized they were bearing the punishment of their previous generations' rebellion against God as well as their own.

Lamentations 5:7 (NIV)
Our fathers sinned and are no more, and we bear their punishment.

Jesus' teaching

This reality is not only illustrated in the lives and stories of the Old Testament; Jesus himself referred to this reality in the gospels. When speaking to the Pharisees and teachers of the law, pointing out their hypocrisy, he talked of grave implications for them and their current generation as a result of previous generations' rejecting, persecuting, and killing the prophets God had sent (a pattern they themselves were now continuing in personally).

Luke 11: 50-51 (NIV)
… and you of this generation will be held responsible for the murder of all God's prophets from the creation of the world – from the murder of Abel to the murder of Zechariah who was killed between the altar and the sanctuary. Yes, it will surely be charged against you.

When the disciples asked Jesus whether a blind man's situation was a result of his own sin or his parents', Jesus did not rebuke them and tell them the biblical principle/reality of generational sin did not apply anymore. He simply said that in that particular situation it was neither due to his nor his parents' sin, but so the work of God might be displayed in his life (Jn. 9:1-5). Jesus was teaching that not all illness is related to generational issues, but He did not deny generational sin.

Apostles' letters

Paul also recognized not only the generational inheritance of sin but also the inheritance of blessing, such as the generational blessing of faith passed down three generations to Timothy by his mother and grandmother.

2 Timothy 1:5 (NIV)
I have been reminded of your sincere faith, <u>which first lived in your grandmother Lois and in your mother Eunice</u> and, I am persuaded, <u>now lives in you also</u> (emphasis added).

THE BIBLICAL PRESCRIPTION FOR GENERATIONAL SIN

It is clear from Scripture that individuals can recognize, take responsibility for, and repent of generational strongholds. Biblical models of this include Ezra, Daniel, Nehemiah and Jeremiah. Each of these men identified with the sin of their ancestors and repented of it, together with their own personal sin.

They each came in humility before God, acknowledging the spiritual principle and reality of generational sin and being obedient to God in applying His prescribed remedy of confession and repentance. They were confident of God's power and mercy to break the effect of the generational sin. Nehemiah not only repented himself but also led the current generation to follow him.

Leviticus 26:14,38,40,42 (NIV)
But if you will not listen to me and carry out all these commands, you will perish among the nations; the land of your enemies will devour you, But if they will confess their sins and the sins of their fathers - their treachery against me and their hostility toward me, I will remember my covenant with Jacob and my covenant with Isaac and my covenant with Abraham, and I will remember the land (emphasis added).

Jeremiah 14:20 (NIV)
O LORD, we acknowledge our wickedness and the guilt of our fathers; we have indeed sinned against you (emphasis added).

Nehemiah 1:6; 9:1 2 (NIV)
Let your ear be attentive and your eyes open to hear the prayer your servant is praying before you day and night for your servants, the people of Israel. I confess the sins we Israelites, including myself and my father's house, have committed against you. On the twenty-fourth day of the same month, the Israelites gathered together, fasting and wearing sackcloth and having dust on their heads. Those of Israelite descent had separated themselves from all foreigners. They stood in their places and confessed their sins and the wickedness of their fathers (emphasis added).

In order to break generational strongholds in our own lives, individuals must humbly follow God's prescribed remedy by repenting of their own sin and on behalf of the sins of previous generations. Since this removes the enemy's right or *topos* in that area, they can then take up their authority in Christ to cut themselves and future generations free from the generational stronghold, just as they would with individual strongholds.

PRESENT EXPERIENCE AND OBSERVATIONS OF GENERATIONAL STRONGHOLDS

The trials and situations people face and often brush off as "normal" may, in fact, be related to generational shadows. There are sins and attitudes that seem so hard to change, however hard they try, even after counseling, self-discipline and behavior modification, etc. The reality is that these issues may be sticking for a reason, because there is a spiritual dynamic that people have not yet understood or addressed. Particular traits that people share with parents and family members such as anxiety, control, or addictive behavior may not just be "coincidence."

This biblical principle of the implications of sin affecting the wider community can be seen not only in family generations but also in the community of a church or even a business. Sometimes we observe a particular pattern of behavior in a church and its people over many years, that continues even when new leaders arrive and old ones move on. There can be a "generational" pattern that is repeated in a church, organization, or business community which we could call a "corporate stronghold." Examples of corporate strongholds over a church could be a religious spirit, independence, financial mismanagement, sexual misconduct, or control/manipulation of power.

Tackling the generational roots of issues in freedom prayer ministry has brought remarkable breakthrough and release to many people and ministries. For a more in-depth understanding of the implications of generational strongholds, and to read testimonies of freedom, please refer to *Living Free: Recovering God's Original Design for Your Life*. You will want to familiarize yourself with these principles and stories in order to be able to explain this important truth to your prayer candidates if and when this issue is exposed as a root of a stronghold in a prayer session.

QUESTIONS REGARDING GENERATIONAL STRONGHOLDS

There are a number of questions that often arise in response to this truth—largely because people are limited by their worldview and lack of exposure to these truths. Most times a simple explanation and reference to Scriptural truth and example will suffice to assure prayer candidates of the biblical truth of what you are presenting.

DO NOT allow the prayer team to be drawn into a theological debate over this issue. If the person does not wish to receive it, simply put that root aside and focus on what he or she is willing to receive at that time.

Some sample questions people often have about generational sin (and some sample responses) are are found in the Appendix . Each of these questions is addressed in greater depth in the book *Living Free: Recovering God's Design for Your Life.* You can refer your prayer candidate to this resource in order to gain a greater depth of understanding on these issues.

DISCERNING AND DISMANTLING GENERATIONAL STRONGHOLDS

There are a number of ways that generational issues might be identified, including personal experience, observation and research of family members, spiritual discernment, and prophetic revelation. For a more thorough treatment of these, please refer to pages 86-87 in The *Living Set Free Course Manual*.

The following is a list (not exhaustive) of symptoms and issues that may be the results of generational sin and strongholds:

- attitudes such as control, insignificance, fear, independence, and rebellion
- witchcraft/occult (including Free-Masonry and similar orders)
- religious sins
- lying, cheating, stealing
- chemical and behavioral addictions *(which can take different forms in different generations)*
- sexual immoralities and abuse
- adultery, pornography
- illegitimate pregnancies
- miscarriages and abortions
- infertility and barrenness
- violence, rage, murder
- physical and verbal abuse
- eating disorders
- gambling
- divorces
- suicide
- infirmities
- anxiety, panic attacks
- depression, mental illnesses
- financial instability, poverty, debt

The trials and situations people face and often brush off as "normal" may, in fact, be related to generational shadows.

DISCERNING A GENERATIONAL STRONGHOLD IN A FREEDOM PRAYER SESSION

When the prayer team is inquiring of the Lord what the roots of a personal stronghold are, one or more of the prayer team may get a sense that the issue is generational. As always, but particularly in this situation, this revelation should be sensitively offered to the prayer candidate. The prayer captain should ask questions, in order to assist the candidate in recognizing it and to ascertain whether the pattern can be seen from his or own experience, knowledge, and observation of the family. In this case, a good general question might be, *"Do you see this pattern of behavior, sin, or attitudes in any other family members?"*

The prayer candidate may immediately recognize it or may struggle to see it. But if he or she gives permission for the prayer team to proceed, then the captain can inquire further of the Lord regarding that generational stronghold, including:

WHICH SIDE OF THE FAMILY?

The prayer candidate may already recognize the family pattern and may know which side the stronghold originates from. In prayer the captain can ask,

"'Lord, from which side of the family was this stronghold passed down?"

The prayer team may get a specific sense regarding either the mother or father's side. It can also be the same sin on both sides of the family that has fortified the stronghold in the person's life.

HOW DID THE STRONGHOLD ORIGINATE?

The captain may inquire, *"Lord, please show us the entry or access point of this stronghold into the family."*

This may come as a picture or word about a specific situation where the stronghold was birthed or started. The picture may be literal or symbolic but it should resonate with identified practice in the family. It is also possible that a listener may receive the number of generations back that the stronghold was started, but this is certainly not necessary to seek out.

> *The purpose of identifying the point of inception is to know how to dismantle the original sin which has given access to the generational sin or curse.*

Again, it is essential at every stage that this revelation is offered sensitively and not forced on the person receiving prayer, giving him freedom to disagree if he feels it is not right. Even if he does not immediately recognize it, however, he may need to act on it in faith. The purpose of identifying the point of inception is to know how to dismantle the original sin which has given access to the generational sin or curse.

WHAT ARE THE RESULTING STRONGHOLDS/SINS?

The captain may ask, *"Lord, what are the strongholds/sins that have come out of this generational sin?"*

For example, if there is a generational stronghold of fear, the Lord may reveal that subsequent sins/strongholds coming out of it (branches, going back to the tree illustration) might be anxiety, sleeplessness, control, and confusion. These will often be sins and/or strongholds the prayer candidate has struggled with himself either in the past or currently. He may be able to identify with some if not all of these.

CORPORATE STRONGHOLDS

Up to this point the focus has been specifically dealing with family generational issues but the process is similar for corporate (or community) strongholds.

If the leader of a church or organization were asking God to bring revelation about corporate strongholds, he or she could follow a similar process for gaining revelation.
- What are the key issues/strongholds being experienced currently in the church/organization?
- Are any of these issues "generational" in the life of the church/organization, extending for years even though individuals come and go?
- Was there a particular inception point for the stronghold, maybe the sin of a previous leader or an incident that happened in the church/organization in the past? (The leader may want to do some research into what happened in the church/organization under previous leaders.)
- What are the resulting sins/strongholds of the main stronghold?

STEPS TO ADDRESSING GENERATIONAL SIN IN PRAYER

People can dismantle generational strongholds in the same way they would any other stronghold, except that they repent not only of their own sin but also of previous generations. The process is very similar to what the prayer candidate has done up to this point and doesn't have to be complex or intimidating.

The steps for addressing generational strongholds are described below and illustrated by a diagram. Start with forgiving previous generations and then continue with the 4R's as you would for any other stronghold. The person receiving prayer can think of himself as "standing in the gap" (Ez. 22:31) between previous generations and Jesus.

FORGIVE

Example: I recognize, ____ (eg Dad) that your actions and attitudes were wrong and hurt me... (own words). You allowed _____ into my life. But today I forgive you. I cancel the debt you owe me and I release you. I also forgive all previous generations on my fathers/mothers side for any way they opened a door to ____.

REPENT on behalf of self and previous generations

Lord Jesus, I repent of where I see this sin in my own life (be specific).

I also repent on behalf of previous generations for the ways in which they have sinned against you (be specific as possible).

I receive your forgiveness and thank you that you have cleansed me completely.

REBUKE cut off generational strongholds in Jesus' name

In the name of Jesus and in His authority I sever and cut off the generational stronghold of ____ from my life and from my future generations. I say that it stops here in Jesus' name. I rebuke the spirit of ____ in my life and command you to leave now in Jesus' name. I break off the lie of ____ and say it no longer has power over me.

REPLACE choose opposite spirit and bless future generations

I replace ____ with ____ (be specific).

I choose to walk in this truth (be specific).

I choose to replace the lies with truth..._____.

I bless future generations with a knowledge of the truth, that they will be people who walk in ____.

RECEIVE God's spirit and empowering

Father, I receive your Holy Spirit and your empowering in order to live in this truth.

Thank you for the freedom you are leading me into.

It may be that the captain needs to lead the prayer line by line if the person receiving prayer is unfamiliar with it. However, if the person has had freedom prayer before and is familiar with using the 4R's, it may be sufficient for the captain to briefly explain each stage and offer a prompt at the start of each section.

FORGIVE

The prayer candidate first grants forgiveness to previous generations for injustices or sins committed. As shown in the diagram, he may wish to picture in his mind that he is facing his predecessors and associated previous generations.

As described in the previous session, he may wish to address his father and/or mother when forgiving him/her. However if the person he is forgiving has passed away it may be more appropriate to address a prayer to God, telling Him he is forgiving that person.

The specific revelation gained will determine whom he needs to forgive and for what.

- **The initial point of entry:** If revelation is received regarding a particular incident or person where the stronghold first entered the family line, the candidate needs to release forgiveness to that person or regarding that situation.

- **Resulting strongholds:** The candidate needs to forgive not only for the main generational sin/stronghold, but also for any resulting sin/strongholds that were received by the prayer team.

Example prayer:

"I recognize, _____(e.g. father/ mother/ grandfather/grandmother) that your actions and attitudes were wrong... (own words). You allowed _____ (sin or stronghold) into our family and into my life. But today I forgive you. I also forgive all previous generations on my father's/mothers' side for any way they opened a door to _____."

THE 4R'S:

1. REPENT

- It may help the prayer candidate to imagine himself turning towards Jesus, with their previous generations stretching out behind him, as shown in the diagram on the previous page.

- The candidate should repent of any way in which he sees the generational stronghold/sin and the resulting strongholds/sins in his own life. He should identify with the sin of previous generations even if he cannot see it obviously in his own life, and repent on behalf of them. He may need to repent on behalf of a specific ancestor regarding the entry point of the stronghold if there has been revelation regarding that.

- Allow a moment for the candidate to receive God's forgiveness and cleansing.

Sample prayer:

"Lord Jesus I repent of where I see this sin in my own life (be specific). I also repent on behalf of previous generations for the ways in which we have sinned against You (be specific if possible). I receive Your forgiveness and thank You that You have cleansed me completely.

2. REBUKE

- The person receiving prayer now takes authority in Jesus' name over any generational stronghold and also any resulting stronghold or sin. He can cut off the generational stronghold cord, and any related lies or curses, in Jesus' name.

- He may wish to imagine turning again to face previous generations to cut the generational cord of the stronghold. He can visualize a cord going from generation to generation, much like an electrical cord through which the enemy energizes the sin. He (or she) may even wish to physically act out cutting the generational cord with his/her arm holding an imaginary sword of the Spirit. This is merely a visual to emphasize the reality and air the candidate's memory.

Sample prayer:

"In the name of Jesus and in His authority I sever and cut off the generational stronghold of _____ from my life and from my future generations. I say that it stops here in Jesus' name. I rebuke the spirit of _____ in my life and command you to leave now in Jesus' name. I break off the lie of _____ and say it no longer has power over me. "

3. REPLACE

- The person receiving prayer may wish to imagine that he is now turning to face future generations.

- He should make a declaration replacing the generational stronghold and resulting strongholds in his own life with the opposite truths and actions, and with specific biblical truths that counter the lies.

- He can also pray a prayer of blessing over future generations (and any children by name if he has any), specifically praying for them to experience and live in the opposite of the stronghold.

Sample prayer:

"I replace _____ with _____ (be specific). I choose to walk in this truth (be specific) _____. I bless future generations with a knowledge of the truth, that they will be people who walk in _____ (identify opposite truths/actions).

4. RECEIVE

- The person prays to receive the Holy Spirit's work in his life to enable him to walk actively in the opposite spirit.

Sample prayer:

"Father, I receive Your Holy Spirit and empowering in order to live in this truth. Thank You for the freedom You are leading me into."

ADDRESSING CORPORATE STRONGHOLDS IN PRAYER

The leader of a church or organization may discern through prayer and observation a pattern or "corporate stronghold." The steps to address corporate strongholds over a church, organization, or business are very similar to those outlined above for family generational issues. Below is a suggested outline of how someone could pray through a corporate stronghold.

FORGIVE: The prayer candidate should forgive previous leaders for any sin/wrong attitudes, and members of the church/organization for any sin/ wrong attitudes.

4R'S:

1. **REPENT:** The leaders should repent on behalf of themselves and previous leaders, and on behalf of members of the church/organization for any sin. Receive God's forgiveness. *(The leaders may also discern that they need to gather together a group of key leaders in the church/organization to corporately repent and intercede on behalf of the wider group/congregation.)*

2. **REBUKE:** They should appropriately declare the delegated authority they have from Christ over the church/organization to break off any corporate strongholds.

3. **REPLACE**: Identify the opposite spirit (e.g. right attitudes and actions) for their lives and the life of the church/organization. Identify any particular changes that need to be made or teaching that needs to be given to help the church/organization walk obediently in the opposite spirit.

4. **RECEIVE**: Ask God for His Holy Spirit to empower the church/organization to live in the opposite spirit.

PRACTICAL EXERCISE: Freedom Prayer for Generational Strongholds

Depending on the time available, today two people in the group will receive prayer concerning a generational stronghold. We will set aside two 30-minute sessions to pray for two people, 30 minutes for each person. We will simply ask the Lord about a generational stronghold He wants to deal with today and ask a few subsequent questions to clarify the revelation.

You may also elect to pray with just one person for one hour, in order to be more thorough; however if you do so, recognize that everyone will not receive prayer this week.

You again will work with an experienced prayer team minister(s) in your group of four. In this portion of the training, one (or two) people will receive prayer concerning generational strongholds. You will join in on the prayer time with the experienced prayer ministers to pray for a person who is on the training course as well.

CONDUCTING THE SESSION

Again, remember to always approach your training prayer sessions as REAL prayer times, not just "practice" sessions. The spiritual transactions your prayer candidates are making are just as significant and important as any other, regardless of the fact that you are all in training.

1. Before you begin your prayer session, remember to:

   - ☑ Prepare the ministry team spiritually.
   - ☑ Seal off the room and the session in prayer, taking authority over any perceived or potential activity of the enemy and inviting the presence of the Holy Spirit.
   - ☑ Greet and prepare your prayer candidate.

(refer to *Freedom Prayer Training Manual "A"* if review is needed on the above procedure)

2. Ask the following questions of the Lord:

- *"Lord, please show us any generational strongholds you wish to deal with in this person's life today, and how they play out in his or her life."*

In today's session let's limit it to one key generational stronghold. If listeners receive more than that, the captain should discern which one to share. Since it is a learning session, the captain may wish to share more than one and discern together with the person receiving prayer which to deal with today.

Once the prayer captain has shared a generational stronghold, if the prayer candidate recognizes the stronghold and is willing to proceed with it, the captain can then ask the Lord the following subsequent questions:

- *"Lord, from which side of the family was this stronghold passed down?"*

- *"Lord, please show us the entry point of this stronghold into the family."*

- *"Lord, what are the strongholds/sins that have come out of this generational stronghold?"* (Try to identify one or two core sin reactions/strongholds and how they play out practically.)

Lead the person through the prayer transaction as previously practiced – forgiveness and then the 4R's (refer to *Freedom Prayer Training Manual "A"*, Session Three).

While the captain is leading the candidate through this prayer, he or she may ask the listeners to listen for pictures and Scriptures related to the truth to replace the specific sin/stronghold/lies, to be shared during the blessing/impartation part of the prayer session.

Pray a prayer of impartation over the person receiving prayer, including specific truths received.

1. As recommended last session, re-read this session after having prayed with your team and a prayer candidate regarding generational attachments. Note any thoughts, impressions, or questions that come up in your mind as you do so.

2. Prepare for the next session of your training by reading Session Ten: Soul-ties.

{ SESSION TEN }
SOUL-TIES: WHAT THEY ARE AND HOW TO MINISTER FREEDOM

Fear of man will prove to be a snare, but whoever trusts in the LORD is kept safe.
Proverbs 29:25

In freedom prayer ministry, one of the most important principles to remember is the same truth the Apostle Paul exhorted us to bear in mind: *"For our struggle is not against flesh and blood*, but against the rulers, against the authorities, against the powers of this dark world and against the spiritual forces of evil in the heavenly realms (Eph. 6:12 NIV, emphasis added).

To put it simply, we live in one world comprised of two realms. While people experience the symptoms of spiritual bondages and affliction in the natural realm, it is important to remember that the roots of those issues are not necessarily in that same realm. If we as prayer teams fail to keep this crucial component of freedom prayer ministry at the forefront of our minds, we risk reducing our prayer times to glorified counseling sessions.

Certain potential spiritual "roots" in particular are so much to the otherworldly end of the spectrum that many believers fail to understand, recognize, or ever deal with their reality in everyday life. "Soul-ties" are one such example. Soul-ties aren't such obvious issues in most people's every day lives as are, say, injustices, love deficits, or generational sin patterns. Unfortunately, they are all too often missed as potential sources of affliction simply because many Christians don't understand or even believe in them—which, of course, makes them even more effective weapons in Satan's arsenal.

In this session, we will address the topic of how to sever the effects of soul-ties through freedom prayer ministry. But first, we need to understand what they are, what they look like, where they come from—and how to help people get free of them.

LEGITIMATE SOUL-TIES

The term "soul tie" is not technically a biblical word, but it does describe a spiritual reality or dynamic. Technically, a soul-tie isn't always bad. The knitting together of people's hearts can bring great blessing when it is a godly relationship. However, it can also bring great destruction when it is an ungodly or unhealthy relationship—which is the focus of our attention in the context of freedom prayer ministry.

Perhaps the best way to understand the biblical concept of a soul-tie is by looking at passages which use the Scriptural terms "cleave" and "knit" (emphasis added):

Genesis 2:24, KJV
Therefore shall a man leave his father and his mother, and shall <u>cleave</u> unto his wife: and they shall be one flesh.

1 Samuel 18:1 KJV
And it came to pass… that the soul of Jonathan was <u>knit</u> with the soul of David, and Jonathan loved him as his own soul.

These passages describe legitimate and healthy "soul-ties" or "soul-bonds" that are part of God's design for life. Some examples of these are spouses to one another, parents and children to one another, close friends, church leaders to those within the local church, and spiritual parents and their "children" to one another.

UNGODLY SOUL-TIES

Even within legitimate biblical relationships, an inappropriate soul-tie can develop. An ungodly soul-tie is a relationship that has transgressed or departed from Biblical guidelines or perimeters for a person in one or more areas, that results in an unhealthy relational bonding or "soul-tie." Such a relationship has an unhealthy, unbiblical influence on the person, family, church, government, or business.

A key aspect of a soul-tie is the inappropriate level of influence between the two individuals. These would be seen by some of the stronghold issues that control an individual's life such as fear, manipulation, selfishness, anger, control, shame, or illegitimate guilt. These ungodly soul ties are spiritual in nature and have the potential to have great power and influence for the enemy's kingdom in a person's life. They not only cultivate debilitating strongholds but can cause confusion, anxiety, unrest, and/or oppression. These kinds of relationships have ceased to be objective.

Examples of unhealthy soul-ties might include:

- controlling parents who discourage their children from leaving home or keep an unhealthy hold over them even though they have left home and/or gotten married
- strong attachment to a past romantic relationship before marriage
- a married man or woman who remains unhealthily attached to his or her parent, trying to please the parent rather than giving his or her spouse the rightful place of priority

Genesis 2:24 (mentioned above) speaks of breaking a soul-tie with one's parents before creating a new godly soul-tie with a spouse. Another example is found in Genesis 44. The relationship between Jacob and his son Benjamin involved an unhealthy soul-tie between them by which Jacob was controlled and influenced in an ungodly way. This is evidenced by Benjamin's brother's comment in Genesis 44:30-31, *"I cannot go back to my father without the boy. <u>Our father's life is bound up in the boy's life</u>. When he sees that the boy is not with us, our father will die. We will be responsible for bringing his grey head down to the grave in sorrow"* (emphasis added).

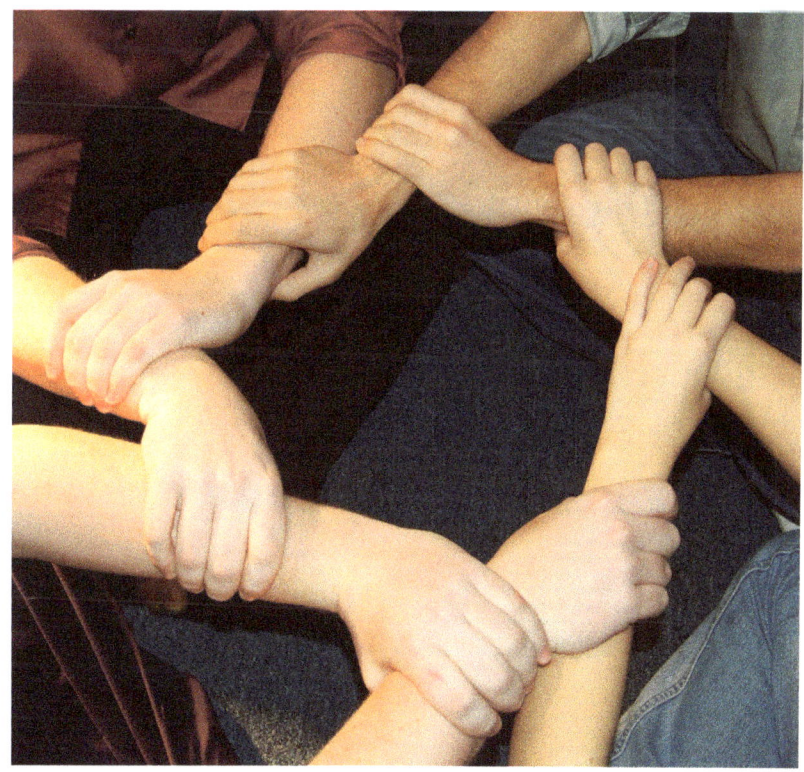

We see another kind of soul-tie—one formed through an inordinate preoccupation with what certain other people think—in Galatians 2, where Paul writes of Peter's hypocrisy. Peter was allowing a fear of what people thought of him to affect his behavior:

Galatians 2:11-13
But when Peter came to Antioch, I had to oppose him publicly, speaking strongly against what he was doing, for it was very wrong. When he first arrived, he ate with the Gentile Christians, who don't bother with circumcision. But afterward, when some Jewish friends of James came, Peter wouldn't eat with the Gentiles anymore because <u>he was afraid of what these legalists would say</u>. Then the other Jewish Christians followed Peter's hypocrisy, and <u>even Barnabas was influenced to join them in their hypocrisy</u> (emphasis added).

HOW UNGODLY SOUL-TIES CAN DEVELOP

Through Misplaced Trust, Fear, and Source of Approval or Identity

This happens when someone is more concerned about, dependent on, or fearful of another person and what he/she thinks than he is of God and what He thinks.

Through Sexual Sin

When sexual activity is involved in a relationship, the strength of a soul tie is increased dramatically. The sexual union between two people ties their souls together as one (Gen. 2:24; 1 Cor. 6:16). When two people are sexually involved with one another their souls literally "cleave" together. It is not only the spoken words of a marriage ceremony which cleaves a couple together into one flesh—it is the physical union. This is why soul ties formed through illicit sexual relationships can be sometimes as strong and binding as those formed through marriage. Because of this reality, this kind of a soul-tie can also be established through any sexual relationship outside of marriage, whether that is premarital sex, promiscuity, adultery, or homosexuality.

Through Spitirual Sin

There can be healthy soul-ties within a church family and between a spiritual leader and the congregation. These can (and should) be a positive connection for the purposes of God in them. However, some spiritual leaders can use their power over followers to control and manipulate. An extreme example would be people in cults who are inappropriately influenced negatively by the leaders and may do things that are destructive to themselves and others out of loyalty to the leaders. A milder form of this would be an extremely charismatic leader who inappropriately influences his followers or congregation by the force of his personality. A third example would be ungodly soul ties formed in occult activities, and oaths and covenants taken in other religions or groups such as freemasonry.

Through Abuses and Violations

Soul ties can be caused by spiritual, mental, emotional, sexual, or physical abuse. It may be the result of abuse over time or a single traumatic event. The abuse can affect the person's mind, emotions, and will so that he or she is overly influenced by thoughts of the person who abused him/her. Fear, sorrow, depression, guilt, addictions, and anger are some of the effects of the spiritual power that this soul tie exerts.

There can be a destructive soul-tie created by sexual violation, for example. Even though the sexual activity was not consensual, there is still a bonding that occurs between people's souls when there is a sexual union. Often the result of this is that the person who has been violated can't seem to stop thinking about the abuser, can't move on and put it behind her (or him). These haunting memories, images, and emotions can follow an individual for the rest of her (or his) life unless the soul-tie is broken.

Through Living in or Grieving about the Past

A soul-tie can develop if a person allows the memories of past relationships, regrets, or a pervading sense of loss to dominate his thoughts and impact his current emotions and relationships. It is right to mourn a loss. However, mourning ought not continue or be excessive as it shuts down the process of receiving God's healing.

MINISTERING FREEDOM

Breaking soul-ties requires that the person receiving prayer recognize them, realize that they are a root of a stronghold and/or enemy activity in his or her life, and desire to be set free. Once this recognition, realization, and desire are established, the prayer team captain can lead the candidate through a prayer to break the soul-tie, receive and extend forgiveness, rebuke the enemy's hold over him or her through the soul-tie, and receive God's power to break free.

When the prayer team receives that a soul-tie is the root of a particular stronghold issue in a prayer candidate's life, the captain should lead the candidate through the following process:

1. IDENTIFY THE SOURCE OF THE SOUL-TIE

The first step is to identify the source or cause of the soul-tie. Point out to the prayer candidate that it is often hard for people to see where their relationships are unhealthy, so we need to ask for God's revelation and allow others to listen and pray with and for us. In addition to asking for Holy Spirit insight, the captain can ask the candidate some probing questions:

- Is there anyone whom you are overly concerned about pleasing?
- Is there is anyone whose presence, if he or she walked into the room now, would cause you to act differently in a negative way?
- Are there previous romantic relationships that still inappropriately influence your thoughts or behavior? Previous sexual relationships?
- Does the opinion of a parent still control you inappropriately?
- Are there are any relationships in which you are controlling or manipulative?
- Is there someone you find it difficult to forgive deeply from your heart?
- Has there been any situation of abuse or violation in your past where a soul-tie may have been created?

The captain may wish to inquire of the Lord for further revelation before proceeding to pray through dismantling the soul-tie and its influence. He can ask the following questions and invite the prayer team to listen for the Holy Spirit's insight:

- With whom is this person connected by a soul-tie?
- What is the source of this soul-tie? (e.g. the person's own sin (sexual, spiritual, occult), misplaced fear/approval, abuse, etc.)
- What or whom does the prayer candidate need to forgive?
- What have been the prayer candidate's sinful responses to this soul-tie?

2. DESTROY THE BONDAGE OF THE SOUL-TIE

How a soul-tie can be dismantled through freedom prayer depends on whether it was developed due to sin or due to being violated.

DISMANTLING A SOUL-TIE ESTABLISHED THROUGH PERSONAL SIN

Using the 4R prayer outline, start with confession of the sin. The prayer candidate should:

 **1. REPENT**

- confess his (or her) own sin which has allowed the soul tie to develop or allowed it to remain
- repent and turn from it (could be sexual sin, involvement in occult, or allowing an unhealthy attachment and allowing oneself to be influenced more by another person than God)

 **2. REBUKE** - Sever the soul-tie

- cut off and sever the soul tie in the blood and authority of Jesus, releasing himself (or herself) from its influence and rebuking any enemy influence that has been given access through it
- renounce any lies, ungodly memories, thoughts, or fantasies

 **3. REPLACE**

- proclaim his or her freedom from the other person's influence and declare his/her decision to be influenced by God
- replace the ungodly thoughts with God's truth and promises
- commit before God to any changes in behavior that will be necessary (for example getting rid of objects relating to occult practice or objects related to a previous relationship, and especially committing to breaking off any sexual relationship that is not under biblical guidelines

4. RECEIVE

- receive God's healing and the filling of the Holy Spirit to empower him or her to walk in freedom and in dependence on God

DISMANTLING A SOUL-TIE ESTABLISHED BY VIOLATION

In this scenario, the prayer candidate should:

FORGIVE
- forgive the perpetrator of the violation or abuse. Be specific about how it made him or her feel. Grant forgiveness, using the principles outlined in Session Five.
- bless the offender(s)
- (Note: Even where there has not been an obvious abuse, the prayer candidate may need to grant forgiveness to a person who has had inappropriate influence over him or her, or has been controlling or manipulative.)

REPENT
- confess any personal sin and sinful reactions including bitterness, resentment, anger, passivity, or control
- repent and turn from the sin

REBUKE, **REPLACE**, and **RECEIVE** as above

1. As recommended last session, re-read this session after having prayed with your team and a prayer candidate regarding soul-ties. Note any thoughts, impressions, or questions that come up in your mind as you do so.

3. Prepare for the next session of your training by reading Session Eleven: Curses.

{ SESSION ELEVEN }
CURSES

I also pray that you will understand the incredible greatness of God's power for us who believe him. This is the same mighty power that raised Christ from the dead and seated him in the place of honor at God's right hand in the heavenly realms.
Ephesians 1:18-20

There are sometimes situations in which sincere believers come to a prayer session experiencing ongoing opposition, frustration, illnesses, and family issues in ways which seem to defy explanation. It would seem that some force is at work—a force that is not simply the usual law of nature and probability. Many times the Lord reveals that a curse is behind a certain situation or stronghold. When the prayer candidate uses the authority of Jesus to renounce the curse and cut it off, very often the situation in his or her life (such as illness or depression) dramatically turns around.

Curses can sometimes be behind believers' experience of the following:

- Repeated or chronic sickness (especially if hereditary)
- Mental and/or emotional breakdown
- Barrenness, a tendancy to miscarry
- Marriage breakdown and family alienation
- Continued financial insufficiency
- High incidence of "accidents"
- Suicides or sucidal tendancies in a family, or unnatural or untimely deaths

Note: It is not being suggested that every calamity or illness is always due to being exposed to a curse or an accursed object. However, in some instances it may be. We need revelation from the Holy Spirit to understand when this is the case and when it is not.

CURSES DEFINED

1. Dictionary

A dictionary definition[4]:

Curse: *Noun*
- a. the expression of a wish that misfortune, evil, or doom would befall a person, group, etc.
- b. a formula or charm intended to cause such misfortune to another
- c. a profane oath; curse word
- d. an evil that has been invoked upon one
- e. the cause of evil, misfortune, or trouble

Curse: *Verb*
- a. to wish or invoke evil, calamity, injury, or destruction upon
- b. to swear at
- c. to blaspheme

2. Encyclopedia

A Bible encyclopedia gives a further explanation: *"A curse was characterized as an entity, a power, force, or energy expressing itself in hurt to be feared and shunned. A curse was not considered a mere wish for misfortune on one's enemies, but a potent force capable of translating pronouncements into tangible results."* [5]

CURSES IN SCRIPTURE

It is important in ministering freedom to people that, when the subject of curses arises, the prayer team (and the captain, in particular) is able to accurately and clearly explain what curses are, why we need to be concerned about them, and the biblical basis and principles for getting free of their influence.

The validity of pronounced blessings and curses in Bible history is clear to see. A few examples are:

- Noah pronounced a curse on Canaan, and a blessing on Shem and Japheth (Gen. 9:25-27) and subsequent history confirmed his invocations.
- The curse invoked by Joshua against anyone who tried to rebuild Jericho was very specifically fulfilled in the life of Hiel who did rebuild the city (Josh. 6:26 and 1 Kin. 16:34).

The Scriptures demonstrate that curses spoken against people have very real impacts on their lives—on their health and on their situations.

> The Scriptures demonstrate that curses spoken against people have very real impacts on their lives—on their health and on their situations.

- In the account of King Balak and an evil prophet called Balaam in Numbers 22-24, the king desperately wanted Balaam to place a curse on Israel for him. God persistently prevented this from occurring; obviously not considering Balaam's words to be empty of power and wanting to protect His people from the significant impact the curse would have on them.

The Scriptures demonstrate that curses spoken against people have very real impacts on their lives—on their health and on their situations. The Bible also illustrates over and over the dangers of curses that come not verbally but through association with unclean or cursed objects, or objects that have been associated with the worship of other gods. For example, many believe that Rachel came under the effects of a curse when she stole her father's household idols—and later died a premature death (Gen. 31:32, 35:19).

2 Corinthians 6:17
Therefore come out from them and be separate, says the Lord. Touch no unclean thing, and I will receive you.

Deuteronomy 7:25-26
The graven images of their gods you are to burn with fire; you shall not covet the silver or the gold that is on them, nor take it for yourselves, or you will be snared by it, for it is an abomination to the Lord your God. You shall not bring an abomination into your house, and like it come under the ban; you shall utterly detest it and you shall utterly abhor it, for it is something banned.

Ezekiel 44:23
Moreover, they shall teach My people the difference between the holy and the profane, and cause them to discern between the unclean and the clean.

TYPES OF CURSES

There are three main types of curses. The first is curses from Satan and/or his servants, the second is from God as a result of disobedience to him and the third type of curses is those spoken by people over each other or over themselves which are then energized by the enemy.

1. Curses from Satan and/or his kingdom

Sadly, there are people today who are committed to furthering the kingdom of Satan through witchcraft and the occult. Curses invoked by these people, and as a result of involvement with objects or activities connected with Satan's kingdom, have significant and real power to bring destruction in people's lives.

2. Curses that are of God

In the Old Testament there are times when the people of God invoked a curse against people who were enemies of God. For example, Joshua spoke a curse against anyone who would try to rebuild the city of Jericho (Josh. 6:26). There are also times in the Old Testament when God pronounced a curse on people who disobeyed or dishonored Him. (Deut. 28 and 29; Mal. 2:2)

With these examples in mind, it appears there may be times when believers are living frustrated lives, thinking that they are opposed by the enemy but actually being opposed by God Himself because of an area of disobedience in their lives. In this case, repentance and obedience are needed rather than spiritual warfare against the enemy's kingdom.

3. Curses from people

This can simply mean being on the receiving end of words from another person which are not godly or pure, causing harm. Often "teasing" is quite acceptable in friendships and families. Unfortunately, these verbal barbs can be an inadvertent source of cursing that can have long-lasting effects. This can include nicknames that have a negative implication, like "klutz" or "Tubby." Many times these can become self-fulfilling prophecies— in effect, curses.

SOURCES/ACCESS POINTS OF CURSES

In order for a curse to impact a person, there needs to be an access point, or a reason why the curse is given authority to "land." The Bible clearly states that "like a fluttering sparrow or a darting swallow, an undeserved curse will not land on its intended victim" (Prov. 26:2). The Bible identifies a number of ways that curses can have access to influence individuals, families, churches, businesses, or even nations.

In order to help people dismantle curses in their lives, we (and they) not only need to understand what forms curses can take, but also the biblically-identified ways in which people can give them authority to "land" and take root in their lives. There are a number of possible access points for curses into our lives. These include generational curses, involvement with unclean or cursed objects, territorial violations, association with occult/demonic rituals/activity, and words energized by the enemy.

Notes:

1. Generational curses

These can be the result of a sin pattern in earlier generations, harsh words or self-fulfilling prophecies spoken over younger generations by previous generations, or activity related to the occult or false religions.[6]

2. Cursed objects and territorial violations

Curses can be given access though involvement with "unclean" or cursed objects or territories, often related to occult practices or demonic idolatry. For example, someone may have entered or violated a physical territory that is under demonic influence, or acted in a disrespectful way towards objects connected with worship of other gods.

Some people may find themselves in possession of objects that have been used in worship of other gods, or in occultic activities. They may own or be in possession of objects which have had a curse placed on them. These objects may have innocently been bought as souvenirs from travels or been inherited from previous generations. Also certain music or movies can have demonic influence, just by their presence in a person's home.

3. Participation in occult or demonic activity

This can include involvement in demonic games, music, films and rituals including Ouija boards, séances, or any other method of seeking direction or protection from Satan's kingdom (e.g. fortune telling, palm reading, tea leaf reading, astrology, etc.).

4. Spoken words and attitudes of people

Words can be powerfully energized by the heavenlies, whether they are blessings or curses. The Bible says that the power of life and death are in words (Prov. 18:21). They can be intentional or unintentional covenants that allow an entry point for the influence of the enemy's kingdom to bring destruction in people's lives.

Word curses may come in the form of harsh words spoken by parents, teachers, other authorities, friends, co-workers and employers, or people with whom people have argued or who are jealous of them. The "word curse" takes root and is energized by the enemy when the person believes it and lives under it. Some examples of spoken word curses might be:

- "Your sister is naturally smart but you'll always have to work for your grades."– sowing fear and striving
- "Good thing for you looks aren't everything."– sowing self-hatred
- "You'll never make anything of yourself."– sowing rejection and insignificance

Other times people can actually curse themselves, saying negative phrases or words about themselves that allow the enemy influence in their lives. Some words might sound like a joke, such as, "I'm so stupid," "Idiot!" or "I'll never be able to do this," *do* have a spiritual impact on people. Some examples of self-inflicted curses might be:

- *"I am not very smart (gifted, talented, skilled, etc). . ."*
- *"I can never be like. . ."*
- *"I will always be poor, . . ."*
- *"I am ugly; no-one would ever want to marry me…"*
- *"I will never be able to…"*

> REMEMBER:
> It is certainly not true that every chronic illness or mental health issue is due to a curse. , it is a matter of in each individual situation inquiring of the Lord and asking Him what proportion of the situation is spiritual (i.e. a curse), and what the source of that curse is. It will be different in each case.

MINISTERING FREEDOM FROM CURSES

You should be able to assure your prayer candidate(s) that Christians need not live in fear or obsession about curses. The enemy would love us to ignorant about it, so we must be aware, but not afraid. When "curse" is received as a root of a stronghold or situation, remind your prayer candidate:

- Greater is God who is in us than Satan who is in the world (1 Jn. 4:4).
- We know that Jesus, in His death and resurrection, destroyed Satan who holds the power of death (Heb. 2:14).
- In Christ, we are more than conquerors (Rom. 8:37).
- We are raised up with Jesus and seated with Him, sharing His authority over the works of the enemy (Eph. 1:19-21, 2:6).
- Therefore, all believers have authority in Christ to break off and render powerless any curses in their lives.

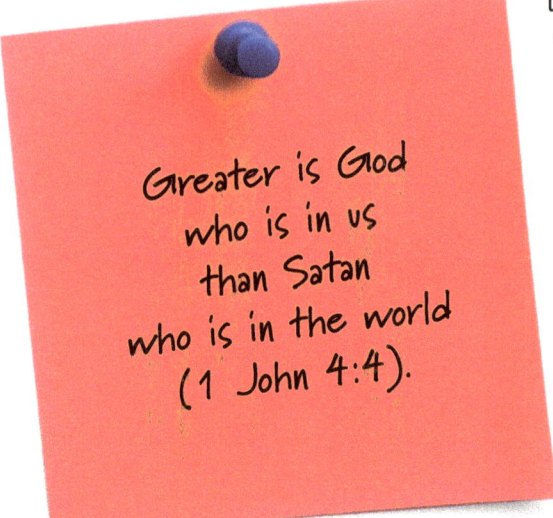

Greater is God who is in us than Satan who is in the world (1 John 4:4).

To minister to someone in response to the revelation that a curse is at the root of a situation or stronghold in the prayer candidate's life, help him or her dismantle any jurisdiction or rightful place the curse has to land. This is done through confession of any sinful activity or attitude (i.e. utilizing the 4-R's) and granting forgiveness toward any who have violated or spoken curses against the prayer candidate. Then the prayer candidate can renounce the curse and free himself or herself, in the power and authority of Jesus, from the curse's influence.

1. Identify the source and access point of the curse

In a freedom prayer session, if a curse has been identified or indicated through revelation or through testimony by the prayer candidate, the captain may wish to ask God for further revelation before proceeding to pray through dismantling the curse and its influence. He or she can inquire of the Lord:

- *What is the source of the curse?* (e.g. Satan's kingdom, disobedience to God, words, etc.)
- *What is the access point of the curse?* (e.g. generational, cursed objects, territorial violations, participation in demonic activity, spoken words, etc.)

Additionally, the prayer team captain may ask the candidate to reflect on (and respond to) the following questions:

- Are there words that were spoken by parents/siblings/teachers/others that were negative and which still seem to be present in your mind, which still hurt and which to some extent you have grown to believe about yourself?
- Are there negative words or phrases that you say about yourself, even if seemingly in jest, in your thoughts or out-loud?
- Are there people with whom you have argued with or people who have been jealous of you (e.g. siblings/business colleagues, etc.) who might have spoken negative words about you?
- Have you ever been involved in any occult activity? (e.g. palm reading, tarot cards, astrology, Ouija board, Wicca, etc)
- Do you have music or movies in your collection that may have any demonic lyrics/content, or about which you feel uneasy?
- Do you own any items/objects that could possibly have been associated with false religions, cults, or occult activity? Are there any items that you have gathered during your travels, or which have been given to you as gifts, about which you feel uneasy?
- Are there any areas of clear and continued disobedience to God in your life?

2. Dismantling Curses

A legitimate curse
(from sin against God or possession of unclean/cursed objects):

Lead the prayer candidate in the following steps:

1. REPENT

- Acknowledge your sin (and any generational sins if necessary), or your possession of unclean/cursed objects. Confess it to the Lord and repent of it.
- Receive God's forgiveness aloud.
- Based on the assurance of God's forgiveness of sin, ask Him to remove the curse that has been placed over your life through your own sin or the association with cursed/occultic objects.

2. REBUKE

- Rebuke any demonic activity and command all demonic beings associated with this curse to be gone, in Jesus' name.

3. REPLACE

- Replace the curse with blessing. Be specific. Receive the Lord's blessing and healing in the particular areas of your life that have been affected by the curse.
- Declare God's protection from all schemes of the enemy, over yourself and your family.
- Commit before God to destroy any items in your possession that are associated with demonic activity or other religions, and follow through with it.

4. RECEIVE

- Verbally acknowledge that you gratefully receive the Holy Spirit's power, enabling, and healing.

An illegitimate curse:

This can include word curses from people spoken against the prayer candidate's life, or curse/activity against him or her from those associated with Satan's kingdom in some way. Lead the prayer candidate in the following:

FORGIVE

- Grant forgiveness to the person(s) as necessary; be specific.
- Bless them.

Notes:

1. REPENT

- Repent of your own reaction to the words (e.g. insignificance, fear, etc.), if appropriate. Repent of believing and living under the lies/word curses (if applicable).
- Receive God's forgiveness.

2. REBUKE

- Speaking out loud, renounce the curse in Jesus' name and command it to be broken.
- Example: *"In the authority of Jesus Christ through His shed blood and resurrection, I take authority over this curse of _____, and command it to be severed and broken now!"*
- Rebuke any demonic activity and command all demonic beings associated with this curse to be gone, in Jesus' name.

3. REPLACE

- Declare God's protection from all schemes of the enemy, over yourself and your family.
- Replace the curse with blessing. Be specific, receiving the Lord's blessing and healing in particular areas of your life

4. RECEIVE

- Receive the Holy Spirit's power, enabling, and healing.

Depending on the time available, today one or two people in the group will receive prayer concerning curses. We will set aside two 30-minute sessions to pray for two people, 30 minutes for each person. We will simply ask the Lord about a curse He wants to deal with today and ask a few subsequent questions to clarify the revelation.

You again will work with an experienced prayer team minister(s) in your group of four. In this portion of the training, one (or two) people will receive prayer concerning curses. You will join in on the prayer time with the experienced prayer ministers to pray for a person who is on the training course as well.

CONDUCTING THE SESSION

Not everyone will be experiencing the effects of a curse in his or her life (although you may be surprised how common this is and how many of us actually are!). If the prayer team does not receive any revelation concerning a curse, the prayer captain can elect to ask a different question covered in a previous session, and have the team pray about that.

1. Before you begin your prayer session, remember to:

    ☑ Prepare the ministry team spiritually.
    ☑ Seal off the room and the session in prayer, taking authority over any perceived or potential activity of the enemy and inviting the presence of the Holy Spirit.
    ☑ Greet and prepare your prayer candidate.

(refer to Session One if review is needed on the above procedure)

2. Ask the following questions of the Lord:

- *"Lord, please show us any curse(s) you wish to deal with in this person's life today, and how it plays out in his or her life."*

The listeners may receive revelation about word curses from others, self-curses, or curses due to sin or unclean objects. The captain should limit it to one or two that will be shared with the prayer candidate. If listeners receive more than that, the captain should discern which one(s) to disclose and deal with. Since this is a training session, the captain may wish to share more than one and discern together with the candidate which to deal with today.

If the prayer candidate recognizes the curse (or even the potential of the curse) and is willing to proceed with it, the captain can then ask the Lord the following subsequent questions:

- *"Lord, what/who is the origin of this curse?*

- *"Lord, please show us the access point that has allowed this curse to 'land.'"*

Lead the person through the prayer transaction as previously practiced – forgiveness (if applicable) and then the 4R's.

While the captain is leading the candidate through this prayer, he or she may ask the listeners to listen for pictures and Scriptures related to the truth to replace the specific curses, to be shared during the blessing/impartation part of the prayer session.

Finally, pray a prayer of blessing and impartation over the person receiving prayer, declaring agreement with what was prayed and including specific truths and words of encouragement that the prayer team received.

1. As recommended last session, re-read this session after having prayed with your team and a prayer candidate regarding curses. Note any thoughts, impressions, or questions that come up in your mind as you do so.

2. Prepare for the next session of your training by rereading any notes you previously took during the course, and any questions that you jotted down. Are there any thoughts, impressions, observations, testimonies you would like to share with the class? Any questions to ask or concepts/practices that need clarification? Take note of these and bring these to the next (and final!) class.

{ SESSION TWELVE }
SUMMARY AND COMMISSIONING

Therefore, I urge you, brothers and sisters, in view of God's mercy, to offer your bodies as a living sacrifice, holy and pleasing to God—this is your true and proper worship. Do not conform to the pattern of this world, but be transformed by the renewing of your mind. Then you will be able to test and approve what God's will is—his good, pleasing and perfect will.
Romans 12:1-2

Congratulations! We have come to the end of our training course. This final session will give you an opportunity to summarize the biblical principles you've learned, ask any outstanding questions, share testimonies with others in your class, and be commissioned into your role as a freedom prayer minister.

After countless experiences of ministering to people in freedom prayer, we have learned something very important: **Freedom prayer ministry is a lifestyle, not a program.** It is living out the mission statement of Jesus, to "proclaim freedom for the prisoners and recovery of sight for the blind, to set the oppressed free, to proclaim the year of the Lord's favor" (Lk. 4:18-29).

We hope the tools and truths you've learned will equip you as the Apostle Paul intended, "for works of service, so that the body of Christ may be built up until we all reach unity in the faith and in the knowledge of the Son of God and become mature, attaining to the whole measure of the fullness of Christ" (emphasis added). Whether you become part of a prayer ministry team in your local church or use this training to better equip you for other areas of ministry, we pray that they become increasingly life-changing—for you and for the people with whom you serve in advancing God's Kingdom.

Share stories with one another during this final class session. Be encouraged as you hear testimonies of how others in your class have experienced—and been vessels of—God's love, truth, and freedom. Be an encouragement to others by sharing your own stories. Together, pray for and affirm one another in your new ministry roles. Finally, receive impartational prayer from your course leaders, commissioning you into a new season of ministry, much in the same way the early church commissioned Barnabas and Saul (Paul) into their new season of ministry:

Acts 13:2-4
While they were ministering to the Lord and fasting, the Holy Spirit said, "Set apart for Me Barnabas and Saul for the work to which I have called them." Then, when they had fasted and prayed and laid their hands on them, they sent them away. So, being sent out by the Holy Spirit, they went down to Seleucia and from there they sailed to Cyprus.

Then celebrate! There's nothing like a celebration to mark the end—and the beginning—of a journey!

{ APPENDIX }

QUESTIONS CONCERNING GENERATIONAL STRONGHOLDS

"HASN'T CHRIST DONE IT?"

People often argue that because of what Christ has done in conquering sin on the cross and through His resurrection, we do not have any relationship to the sins of the past – either our own or those of our families and communities before us.

It is true that when we receive Christ as our Savior, the guilt of our sin is washed away by His sinless sacrifice and we are made new (2 Cor. 5:17; Col. 2:13; Rev. 1:5). Our position before God is absolutely righteous, without any condemnation, because we are in Christ (Rom. 8:1).

However, we need to make a distinction between a believer's sin being dealt with on a judicial or "legal" basis and its practical ramifications. Even though we have been forgiven, we still have to address the practical consequences of our sin. Our sin is dealt with *legally* by the cross of Jesus but it is still possible to live under the *practical* effects of it. We need to actively appropriate the power of Christ's death and resurrection not only regarding our own individual sin and strongholds, but also for any generational patterns and strongholds by which we may be affected.

"WASN'T THAT LEFT BEHIND IN THE OLD TESTAMENT?"

Other questions which often arise stem from texts such as Ezekiel 18, which appear at first reading to say that bearing responsibility of past generations has ceased. In fact, at closer reading of the text, in the context of Ezekiel's prophecies and of the rest of the Bible, it seems that is not exactly what Ezekiel was saying.

In this passage, God was not saying that the spiritual dynamic of generational sin was no longer in effect. He was simply stating the principle that had already been established in Scripture: that the ongoing effects of generational sin can be broken by a generation taking responsibility for and repenting of its own sin and that of previous generations.

"IF I TACKLE A GENERATIONAL ISSUE, DOES THAT FREE THE REST OF MY FAMILY?"

Many people ask whether, when they have broken a generational stronghold, will this have an impact in freeing other members of their family. This is an important question and to answer it, it is important to understand the biblical truths about God's government or delegated authority.

Generational strongholds in families

If Christian parents of young children are repenting of and renouncing a generational stronghold, they can do so on behalf of their children as well, as they still have spiritual authority over their children. They can set up a new pattern of blessing and truth in their own lives, pray that into their children's lives, and practically apply the opposite spirit in the family life.

However, if children are adults (or close to it), they may need to deal with their own sin before God and tackle the generational stronghold themselves. It does no harm for the parent to pray the opposite spirit into an adult child's life but there will be aspects of it for which the adult child must take personal responsibility before God. If appropriate, the parents can set the example by confessing their own sin to their children, asking for their forgiveness, and explaining how they, too, can sever the effects of generational sin from their lives.

If an adult child is breaking a generational stronghold from his life, this doesn't necessarily free his parents from the effects of the stronghold. The parents may need to take responsibility and tackle the issue in their own lives before God. However, it can be powerful for the child to intercede for the parents (and any siblings or other family members), asking for God to release them from the stronghold or for the chains to be loosened sufficiently for them to be able to see it and address it themselves.

Corporate strongholds in churches or organizations

Similarly, when praying about corporate strongholds in a church, an understanding of God's government and the structure of delegated authority is necessary. The leaders of a church have delegated authority from God over the church and as such can repent on behalf of themselves and the church, and in Jesus' authority break the corporate stronghold in prayer. They would then need to walk and act in the opposite spirit, to set up new patterns of obedience and blessing. The leaders also have responsibility for leading and teaching the church about the danger of the stronghold that had been established in the life of the church. If appropriate, they should lead the church in corporate repentance and certainly in teaching and modeling how to walk in the opposite spirit.

A member of a church who is not the leader would not have the authority to sever corporate strongholds from the whole church. However, it would be powerful for that person to repent of any way he sees it in his own life, start to walk in the opposite spirit, and to intercede for the leaders and for the church, asking God to reveal the stronghold to them and bring repentance and freedom.

"I DON'T WANT TO 'CUT OFF' MY PARENTS – THEY ARE GOOD PEOPLE"

Severing generational strongholds does not mean cutting off the positive connections people have with their parents and previous generations. Breaking the power of generational sin merely means cutting off any influence the enemy has had in passing down sin/strongholds through the family. It is important to emphasize to people that they are not "cutting off" their parents completely, and that they can still be assured of a godly connection with their parents.

STRONGHOLDS LISTED AND DESCRIBED

1. Strongholds of PASSIVE Reaction (Defeatism)

1a APATHY

- It is simply an attitude of inactivity, being resigned, no initiation.
- It can blossom out of both rejection and rebellion, but none-the-less it puts us in the place Satan wants the Christian to live.
- Jesus said that it is with violence that the Kingdom of God is received.

1b VICTIMIZATION

- Deceptive, and will gather onlookers, sympathizers, and empathizers.
- Most of the time it is wrongly comforted instead of being confronted.
- This is cultivated soil for offences.

1c SELF-HATRED

- This is a more severe step than self-pity.
- Abusive relationships and situations are an open door for this spirit.
- This is expressed in addictive behaviors, sexual perversions, and general disregard for one's life and relationships.
- This stronghold imprisons one into believing that his or her purpose and identity are linked to appearance, and that one's beauty is in our outward appearance.

1d INFERIORITY

- It believes that we are lower in value and significance than others.
- It believes that we are low grade, second class, substandard, not measuring up to others.
- Many times this stronghold causes someone to see himself or herself as a failure.
- Many things are associated with inferiority, such as self-pity, jealousies, over-achieving, etc

1e SHAME/CONDEMNATION

- Not the positive guilt that is a warning system that keeps us from straying from the truth that God desires us to live by that brings health.
- This is living perpetually with painful feelings of guilt for improper behavior.
- This can be associated with acts committed by a person as well as abuse committed against a person.
- This many times is carried in response to something hidden or kept in secret.

1f INSECURITY

- This is rooted in fear of not being accepted, loved, or approved.
- It is thinking that whoever the Lord created us to be is not good enough.
- This promotes not only unhealthy attitudes and actions toward one's self, but toward others in various ways.
- Must return to seeing one's self as God sees.

1g HOPELESSNESS

- Perceives life with no possibility for success, overcoming, and/or solution.
- One lives in despair.
- It resides with unbelief and passivity.

1h DEPRESSION

- Can be an accumulative effect of love deficit.
- Can be related to a direct and specific traumatic loss or situation.
- Its source can be the guilt of sin.
- Again, the source must be identified and addressed, not the symptom.

1i SUICIDE

- Associated with strongholds/spirits of death and destruction.

2. Strongholds of AGGRESSIVE Reaction ("I'll show you!!!")

(Note: Usually those with rebellion issues struggle a little bit around leadership, or in their relationship to leadership, and will wrestle with authority issues.)

2a CRITICAL

- A critical spirit looks at people and circumstances from a negative perspective. It is impatient, irritable, and inflexible with others instead of having grace, kindness, mercy, patience, understanding, charity, and benevolence.
- This stronghold points out weaknesses and idiosyncrasies with a view to tear down versus build-up.
- Friends, family, co-workers, church-family, situations, and others around you are criticized with a view to tear down versus build-up.

2b BITTERNESS/RESENTMENT/UNFORGIVENESS

- This stronghold carries with it extreme enmity, sharpness, harshness, and spite. There is a feeling of indignation from being injured, violated, or offended.
- To forgive means to give up the desire, or to not exercise the right, to punish; to give up all claim to exact penalty; to pardon, cancel, and release.

2c HOSTILITY/HATRED

- To harbor ill-will, antagonism, great dislike and aversion, and hostile dislike.
- This too is related to the issues of forgiveness.

2d SUPERIORITY/SELF-EXALTING/CONCEIT: (INCLUDED AND ASSOCIATED WITH THIS ARE PRIDE, ARROGANCE, ETC.)

- This is an aggressive expression of inferiority.
- It is an issue of establishing one's significance, and cloaking the pain of inferiority.
- Over-achieving is often related to this brick, as well as that of competitive.

2e PRIDE/CONCEIT

- This is exaggerated self-esteem, haughtiness, arrogance, a self-flattering opinion of one's self, self-important, independent.
- to be self-absorbed, selfish
- to one's self as more important than others
- to view one's self and interests above others
- to put my trust in me, my capacities, my position, my deeds instead of God.

2f COMPETITIVE

- There is healthy competition, but not one that derives one's self-worth and value.
- This many times is the result of performance-based love, which is another form of "love deprivation." The love they received was not purely out of a love for them as a person, but what they could do or become.
- Selfish ambitions, perfectionism, "climbing to the top" are some of the expressions of such a stronghold.

2g CONTROL/STUBBORN/MANIPULATION

- Many times because of wounds, one takes an aggressive role to protect himself or herself from further hurts by seeking to control the situations and relationships in his or her life.
- Control, domination, manipulation, and etc. strip us from emotion (except anger in which many contend is not an emotion).
- Control, domination, manipulation, and etc. is rooted in fear.
- The stubborn have to be right or it has to be done his or her way, again to control.
- The unteachable find their control, identity, significance in knowledge.

2h JEALOUSY/COVETOUS

- Demanding exclusive loyalty, resentfully envious, desirous and eager to obtain, inordinate desire, jealously seeks to obtain or possess, to grasp for, greed.
- It is discontent with, and even despising that which God has given.
- It many times nurtures anger and resentment.
- It feeds competition.
- It is self-focused and causes to withhold blessings, affection, and words & actions of encouragement to others.

2i ANGER

- Note: anger is a secondary emotion, meaning that it is a reaction to and/or expression of a primary emotion such as bitterness, hostility, resentment, and etc. that come from wounds and/or love deprivation.
- These emotions are aggressive responses to love and truth deprivation in our lives.
- Anger and associated emotions cause turmoil in one's inner person and other relationships and situations in his or her life.
- Unforgiveness and anger go hand in hand.

2j BETRAYAL/MURDER

- To violate trust, to break faith by disclosing a secret or anything that had been given in trust, to mislead or lead astray, to delude or ensnare, to damage and destroy.
- Many times comes out of personally receiving an offense or rejection, not necessarily from those whom the person betrays.
- Sometimes done out of insecurities and inferiority to gain position, recognition, wealth, and/or influence.
- The seed of betrayal/murder can be found in rebellion, anger, offense, jealousy, independence, preeminence, discontent, and ambition.

ENDNOTES

1. Mike Riches and Tom Jonez, *Hearing God's Voice for Yourself and Others*, SycPub Global, Gig Harbor, WA: 2010.
2. This section on impartation contributed by Arlyn Lawrence.
3. Arlyn Lawrence and Cheryl Sacks, *Prayer-Saturated Kids*, NavPress: Colorado Springs, CO: 2007.
4. www.dictionary.com. Based on the *Random House Dictionary*, Random House, Inc.: New York, New York, 2010.
5. Merrill C. Tenney, ed., *The Zondervan Pictorial Encyclopedia of the Bible*, (Grand Rapids; Zondervan, 1975).
6. For a more thorough treatment of generational curses, please refer to *Living Free: Recovering God's Original Design for Your Life* by Mike Riches, SycPub Global: Gig Harbor, WA, 2008, 2011.

ABOUT THE AUTHOR

Dr. Michael (Mike) D. Riches, D.Div. has served as a lead pastor for over 40 years, and is currently in full-time pastoral ministry, along with his wife, Cindy, in Gig Harbor, Washington, where he serves as lead pastor of Harborview Fellowship.

Since 2001, Mike has ministered around the United States and overseas as the Founder and Director of The Sycamore Commission (www.sycamorecommission.org), a growing international teaching and equipping ministry committed to the support and reformation of the Church. Believing strongly that Jesus intended for His mission to continue with His disciples both then and now, the focus of the Sycamore Commission's ministry is to serve the Body of Christ by helping church leaders, churches, and individual Christians understand, fully recover, and live out the powerful, life-changing, Kingdom-advancing ministry of Jesus Christ.

Mike's ministry involves teaching, training, leadership development and support, and freedom prayer training. He has authored *Living Free: Recovering God's Design for Your Life, Living Set Free in Christ, Walking in Freedom, Foundations of Freedom,* and *Hearing God's Voice for Yourself and Others (*co-authored with Tom Jonez).

Also from SycPub Global:

LIVING SET FREE IN CHRIST

The *Living Set Free in Christ* course manual—as part of the *Living Set Free* course— will help you experience and enjoy the freedom and favor that is found only through Jesus Christ, including topics like: God's original design for your life and His unconditional love for you, how to completely release past hurts and injustices, how to exercise your spiritual authority, how to break the power of spiritual strongholds and generational sin patterns from your life, and much more.

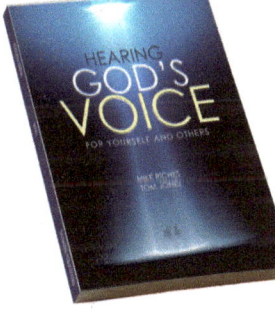

FOUNDATIONS OF FREEDOM

Foundations of Freedom is a five-session experience of the larger *Living Set Free in Christ* course (which is 12 one-hour sessions), and is suitable for use in workshops, small-groups, and one-on-one discipleship settings, as well as for personal devotional use. It provides a primer on starting on a path to freedom in Jesus Christ, equipping you with the biblical truth you need in your pursuit of living the abundant life Jesus promised..

HEARING GOD'S VOICE FOR YOURSELF AND OTHERS

In this illustrated, full-color manual, you'll learn powerful truths and principles for returning to God's biblical normal for communicating with Him. Includes practical assignments for group or class study.

WALKING IN FREEDOM

Designed to accompany the *Living Set Free in Christ* course manual, *Walking in Freedom* will help you practically apply spiritual transactions that result in freedom from particular bondages in your life. Through Christ's power and the simple steps outlined in this book—including diagnostic inventories that help identify if and how certain strongholds might exist in your life— you can break out of specific bondages and walk in the freedom Jesus purchased for you.

Order at www.sycpubglobal.com

www.ingramcontent.com/pod-product-compliance
Lightning Source LLC
Chambersburg PA
CBHW061812290426
44110CB00026B/2857